Divergent Thinking

for **ADVANCED LEARNERS**

Grades 3–5

Divergent Thinking for Advanced Learners, Grades 3–5 will develop students' specific creative thinking skills.

Divergent thinking is a skill which helps students approach problems with a flexible and open mind. Working through the lessons and handouts in this book, students will learn to examine problems from multiple perspectives and fluently generate varied solutions. This curriculum provides cohesive, scaffolded lessons to teach each targeted area of competency, followed by authentic application activities for students to then apply their newly developed skill set.

This book can be used as a stand-alone gifted curriculum or as part of an integrated curriculum. Each lesson ties in both reading and metacognitive skills, making it easy for teachers to incorporate into a variety of contexts.

Emily Hollett and **Anna Cassalia** are award-winning gifted educators and instructional differentiation coaches with Williamson County Schools, Tennessee.

Discover the other books in the Integrated Lessons in Higher Order Thinking Skills series

Available from Routledge
(www.routledge.com)

Analytical Thinking for Advanced Learners, Grades 3–5
Emily Hollett and Anna Cassalia

Convergent Thinking for Advanced Learners, Grades 3–5
Emily Hollett and Anna Cassalia

Evaluative Thinking for Advanced Learners, Grades 3–5
Emily Hollett and Anna Cassalia

Visual-Spatial Thinking for Advanced Learners, Grades 3–5
Emily Hollett and Anna Cassalia

Divergent
Thinking

for **ADVANCED**
LEARNERS

Grades 3–5

Emily Hollett
and
Anna Cassalia

Routledge
Taylor & Francis Group

NEW YORK AND LONDON

Cover image: © Educlips

First published 2023
by Routledge
605 Third Avenue, New York, NY 10158

and by Routledge
4 Park Square, Milton Park, Abingdon, Oxon, OX14 4RN

Routledge is an imprint of the Taylor & Francis Group, an informa business

© 2023 Emily Hollett and Anna Cassalia

Library of Congress Cataloging-in-Publication Data
Names: Hollett, Emily, author. | Cassalia, Anna, author.
Title: Divergent thinking for advanced learners (grades 3–5)/Emily Hollett, Anna Cassalia.
Description: New York, NY: Routledge Press, 2022. |
Series: Integrated lessons in higher order thinking skills | Includes bibliographical references. |
Identifiers: LCCN 2022002640 (print) | LCCN 2022002641 (ebook) |
ISBN 9781032213484 (hardback) | ISBN 9781032199245 (paperback) |
ISBN 9781003267959 (ebook)
Subjects: LCSH: Divergent thinking–Study and teaching (Elementary) | Critical thinking in children. | Metacognition in children. | Gifted children–Education (Elementary)
Classification: LCC LB1590.3 .H666 2022 (print) | LCC LB1590.3 (ebook) |
DDC 371.95–dc23/eng/20220224
LC record available at https://lccn.loc.gov/2022002640
LC ebook record available at https://lccn.loc.gov/2022002641

ISBN: 978-1-032-21348-4 (hbk)
ISBN: 978-1-032-19924-5 (pbk)
ISBN: 978-1-003-26795-9 (ebk)

DOI: 10.4324/9781003267959

Typeset in Warnock Pro
by Deanta Global Publishing Services, Chennai, India

Access the Support Material: www.routledge.com/9781032199245

We would like to dedicate this book to all the students we've taught and will teach. You are the reason why we love this profession and wrote this series. We would also like to dedicate this series to our families, who have supported us unconditionally.

Contents

Contents

Acknowledgments

Special credit and acknowledgment must go to the many individuals whose work has paved the way for current educators like ourselves.

We draw great inspiration from the work of Sandra Kaplan, Alex Osborn, Sydney Parnes, Tony Wagner, Tamra Stambaugh, and Joyce VanTassel-Baska, whose curricular frameworks and research into best practice for teaching gifted learners are a driving force in shaping our own work.

Our guiding principles are grounded in National Association for Gifted Children (NAGC) programming standards, and we are so thankful for this organization's tireless dedication to gifted students, advocacy, and lifelong learning.

Clipart courtesy of Educlips. Used with permission under an extended license for hard copy books.

Handout font courtesy of Kimberly Geswein. Used with permission under a single font license.

Preface

The *Integrated Lessons in Higher Order Thinking Skills* series provides explicit instruction, targeted problems, and activities to teach gifted and high-ability students how to think using convergent, divergent, analytical, evaluative, and visual-spatial reasoning.

This unit was developed by and for teachers of gifted and advanced learners to provide explicit instruction in higher order thinking skills. In today's ever-changing, fast-paced world, our students require skill sets beyond rote memorization. Vast research supports the development of higher order thinking skills, including both creative and critical thinking skills which go beyond basic observation of facts and memorization. Systematically teaching these processes to students develops their ability to use these skills across the curriculum, building their ability to be "thinkers"—the ultimate goal of education.

The term "21st Century Thinking Skills" is widely used in education today, and while definitions vary, most educators agree: we need to be teaching our students not just *what* to think, but *how* to think. Learners in the 21st century must possess an array of thinking skills. They must be inquisitive about the world around them, and willing to ask questions and make mistakes. They must be logical and strategic thinkers. Logical thinking requires students to clarify problems while analyzing and making inferences based on the given information. Strategic, or deliberate, thinking requires students to think about where they are now in the learning process versus where they want to be in the future, and then determine action steps to achieve their goals.

Gifted and high-ability students require specialized instruction which is organized by key concepts and overarching themes. They need content which requires abstract thinking on a higher level than what is typically required by the general education curriculum. Beyond this, they require time to grapple with meaningful problems and derive defensible solutions. The *Integrated Lessons in Higher Order Thinking Skills* series provides scaffolded, focused lessons to teach these skills and give students authentic opportunities to develop these vital thinking processes.

Rationale

As Tony Wagner (Wagner and Compton, 2012) noted, our current educational system is obsolete and failing to educate our youth for the world of tomorrow. Wagner (Wagner and Compton, 2012) stated, "Students who only know how to perform well in today's educational system—get good grades and test scores and earn degrees—will no longer be those who are most likely to succeed. Thriving in the twenty-first century will require real competencies far more than academic credentials" (p. 20). Our educational system must help our youth discover their passions and purpose in life, and then develop the crucial skills necessary to think critically and creatively, communicate effectively, and problem-solve (Wagner and Compton, 2012).

Developing 21st-century thinkers requires a classroom environment that welcomes cognitive discourse and embraces the growth mindset approach. We must also teach our students that it is acceptable not to have an immediate answer; that some questions have many possible solutions, and indeed, some may never be answered; that persevering and being able to admit what you don't know is an important piece of learning.

Today's students must use metacognition, or awareness of and reflection on thinking processes. Metacognitive thinking is abstract in that one must analyze their thinking processes. Examples of this type of thinking might be asking oneself: "How did I get to that answer?" or "Where did my thinking go off track?" Learning to analyze the process of thinking is vital to problem-solving and learning. Teaching metacognitive strategies is a powerful way to improve students' self-efficacy, depth of thinking, and inquiry skills.

Students of the 21st century must develop problem-solving skills which require both creative and critical thinking. Creativity is a divergent thought process which involves generating new and unique possibilities. Critical thinking is a thought process which involves examining possibilities using a systematic, constructive method. Our students will be faced with unforeseen challenges that they must be able to think about creatively, critically, and strategically to solve. We, as educators, cannot possibly teach students everything there is to know, as the amount of new information available in the world is multiplying rapidly. Therefore, we must teach students to be inquisitive, analytical, innovative, evaluative, and curious. Learning and applying these thinking skills will prepare our students to solve the problems of tomorrow.

While we know the importance of higher order thinking, it is often left behind the "testable subjects" such as reading, writing, and arithmetic. This series was created to merge higher order thinking skills and the academic content students must grapple with in school. Systematic instruction in higher order thinking skills coupled with rigorous academic content is a relevant and engaging method to teach the students of the 21st century.

Higher order thinking consists of several distinctive and sophisticated thought processes. Central to these processes are the areas of systematic decision making (deductive reasoning), evaluative thinking, divergent (creative) thinking, concept attainment, and rule usage (analytical). In addition, visual-spatial reasoning has emerged as one of the most important skills for developing overall academic expertise, especially in technical fields. Each of these central processes is addressed in its own book within the *Integrated Lessons in Higher Order Thinking Skills* series.

Focus Strand: Divergent Thinking

This book focuses on one specific strand of higher order thinking: divergent thinking. Divergent thinking is the ability to think creatively, outside the confines of standard expectations. The four main indicators of divergent thinking are fluency, flexibility, originality, and elaboration. Each of these indicators encompasses a specific aspect of creative thinking, and research tells us that each of these facets can be taught and developed. Learning divergent thinking skills helps students approach problems with an open mind and withhold judgment before arriving at solutions. Thinking creatively forces students to use strategies to elaborate and combine ideas to create something new and original. Divergent thinkers learn to look flexibly at problems from multiple perspectives and fluently generate many and varied solution ideas. Divergent thinking requires developing an intentional purpose and a targeted plan of action to make ideas come to life. Utilizing divergent thinking, students uncover unforeseen ideas and solutions when solving challenging problems.

This book breaks down divergent thinking into five distinctive sub-skills: generating ideas, changing perspectives, elaborating, innovating, and giving ideas purpose. Each of these skills is taught explicitly through three lessons, increasing in complexity and abstraction, and culminating in an application lesson and activity. This approach allows students to build their divergent thinking skills incrementally and apply each skill as it develops. By completing all lessons in this book, students will be able to apply divergent thinking skills and strategies to a variety of problems, situations, and contexts.

Conceptual Framework

This curriculum is targeted for third through fifth grade gifted and high-ability students. Frameworks for questioning and methodology were drawn from several research-based sources, including the Depth and Complexity Framework (Kaplan and Gould) and the Osborn-Parnes Creative Problem-Solving (CPS) Process.

Working through the lessons in this book, students will make connections by thinking in ways that incorporate elements of the Depth and Complexity Framework, such as thinking like a disciplinarian, connecting to universal themes, reasoning using question stems derived from the icons/elements, and examining problems through the lens of the content imperatives.

Students will develop creative thinking skills based upon elements of the original Creative Problem-Solving Process which was linear in nature (Osborn and Parnes), and using various adaptions to the CPS model which made it more fluid (Isaksen, Dorval, and Treffinger). In addition, students will learn a variety of thinking tools to aid in generating and focusing their ideas through brainstorming (Osborn), SCAMPER (Eberle), force-fitting, and the evaluation matrix (Isaksen, Dorval, and Treffinger). These research-based frameworks are embedded within the lessons in the form of question stems, instructional processes, graphic organizers, and methodology.

Each unit in the series uses explicit instruction to directly and systematically teach students how to think with a specific thinking process. Research shows that the most empirically supported method for teaching critical thinking is explicit instruction (Abrami, Bernard, Borokhovski, Wade, Surkes, Tamim, and Zhang, 2008). Using explicit instruction makes the learning outcomes clear.

Students are provided with clear, specific objectives. The unit lessons are broken down into manageable chunks of information. The teacher models the thinking skill with clear explanations and verbalizes their thinking process. Students are taught specific ways to reason and problem-solve. Students then practice the skills while the teacher provides feedback. At the conclusion of each lesson, students are asked to think metacognitively about their own learning.

Lesson Format and Guidelines

Each *Integrated Lessons in Higher Order Thinking Skills* unit follows the same format. Students are introduced to the higher order thinking skill through introductory lessons and materials to build schema in the targeted thinking area addressed in the unit. The introductory lesson in each unit provides a real-world connection. The overarching thinking skill is then broken down into five sub-skills. Each sub-skill is explicitly taught in three lessons. First, the students will be introduced to the sub-skill using an anchor chart. Then, students will participate in a warm-up activity teaching the sub-skill. Next, students will read and analyze trade books which highlight the sub-skill. Finally, students will participate in an activity learning to use the sub-skill. The third lesson in each sub-skill provides an opportunity for the students to apply the sub-skill in an authentic application activity. Key features of this unit as well as lesson summaries are outlined in Table P.1.

Unit Features

Materials

Included in this book are blackline masters of consumable materials to be used with students. Student handouts are provided with each lesson, and they include reading reflections, graphic organizers, full text stories for collaborative learning activities, formative "exit tickets," and others. Teacher materials, including anchor chart posters to provide visual cues for sub-skills, detailed lesson plans, and assessment rubrics, are also included. Other needed and optional materials are listed in lesson outlines. Links are provided for online resources, such as short video clips, and are accurate at the time of this book's printing.

Throughout the unit, trade books are used to teach and explore sub-skills in familiar contexts. These carefully selected trade books provide an exemplar for the lesson's focus. The recommended books are common and easily accessible; however, alternate texts are recommended to target each sub-skill (see Appendix B). Many of the texts may also have a digital version readily available as an online read aloud, accessible through a quick internet search.

In addition, some lessons utilize common classroom manipulatives such as attribute blocks, pattern blocks, or Tangrams. Printable versions of these manipulatives are also provided as handouts where they are used.

Teacher's note: It is always recommended that teachers preview any content (books, videos, images, etc.) before implementing it with students. Be sure to consider the context of the classroom and/or school in which the materials

TABLE P.1
Unit Overview

Introduction and Rationale Teacher introduction providing rationale for the unit.	❏ Outline of Thinking Skills: Teacher reference explaining an overview of each thinking skill and outcome. ❏ Standards Alignment: Unit alignment to both CCSS and NAGC standards are outlined.
Thinking Skill Overview This section provides introductory lessons and materials to build schema for students in the specific targeted thinking skill addressed in the unit.	❏ Frame of the Discipline: Think Like an Artist 　■ Students gain understanding of authentic uses for divergent thinking skills within a career context. ❏ Artwork Analysis: Students analyze a piece of classic visual art through the lens of divergent thinking to build thinking skill schema. ❏ Thinking Skills Avatar: Provides an ongoing touch-stone for students to record key details and synthesize learning throughout the unit.
Sub-Skill 1: Generating Ideas In this section, students will learn to fluently generate many and varied ideas to develop the skill of flexible thinking.	❏ Lesson 1: Avoiding Judgment 　■ Students learn to avoid judgment and fluently generate multiple ideas. ❏ Lesson 2: Developing Fluency 　■ Students will practice stretching their minds to combine and connect multiple ideas. ❏ Authentic Application Activity: Force-Fitting Ideas Together 　■ Students apply brainstorming to solve a problem by generating and/or combining multiple ideas.
Sub-Skill 2: Changing Perspectives In this section, students will consider multiple perspectives, develop flexibility in thinking, and examine various viewing angles in exploring a variety of novel scenarios.	❏ Lesson 1: Looking at Different Visual Perspectives 　■ Students will consider visual images from a variety of angles, evaluating how the angle of viewing alters perspectives. ❏ Lesson 2: Understanding Others' Points of View 　■ Students will evaluate the perspectives of others, considering similarities to and differences from their own perspectives. ❏ Authentic Application Activity: Circle of Viewpoints 　■ Students will consider scenarios from various characters' viewpoints to analyze a problem using multiple perspectives.

(Continued)

TABLE P.1
(Continued)

Sub-Skill	Content
Sub-Skill 3: Elaborating In this section students work in cross-curricular contexts to develop ideas and solutions through elaboration.	❏ Lesson 1: Visual Elaboration ■ Students explore adding details to visual art to discover the impact of elaboration. ❏ Lesson 2: Elaborating in Writing ■ Students will create a shared writing piece, focusing on adding details to make the story more interesting and complete. ❏ Authentic Application Activity: Using Elaboration in Opinion Writing ■ Students will write an opinion piece with a focus on elaborating with detailed reasoning and supporting evidence.
Sub-Skill 4: Innovating Students will generate new, unique, and original ideas through collaboration and modification of existing ideas to create new and original products.	❏ Lesson 1: Discovering New Uses ■ Students will combine and modify common classroom items to develop new uses for objects. ❏ Lesson 2: Innovating with Existing Ideas ■ Students will learn the SCAMPER idea-generating tool as a framework for innovation in thinking. ❏ Authentic Application Activity: Creating a Purposeful Innovation ■ Students will independently use the SCAMPER technique, creating an innovation while considering its functionality and benefits.
Sub-Skill 5: Giving Ideas Purpose Students work to refine ideas in purposeful, authentic contexts by exploring action plans, audiences, and limitations of solutions.	❏ Lesson 1: Setting an Intentional Purpose ■ Students will consider purpose and audience in developing a new idea. ❏ Lesson 2: Creating a Plan of Action ■ Students will develop action plans to accomplish solution paths. ❏ Authentic Application Activity: Creative Problem-Solving ■ Students will learn the steps of the Creative Problem-Solving framework and then apply it to a fairytale problem.
Appendix A **Appendix B**	❏ Assessment Options ❏ Extension Options

are to be used, being sensitive to the needs, experiences, and diversity of the students.

Assessments

Possible solutions and suggested key understandings are provided throughout the unit. These sample answers were created to help the teacher see the intended purpose for each lesson and illustrate the thinking skills students should be mastering. However, due to the open-ended nature of many of the lessons and activities, these answers should only be used as a guide and variations should be encouraged.

Blackline masters of assessment options are provided in Appendix A. Formative assessments are provided throughout the unit in the form of an exit ticket to conclude each sub-skill section. An overall unit rubric is provided along with diagnostic guidelines for observation. A whole-group checklist is provided for each sub-skill with diagnostic guidelines included. Teachers should review and select assessment options that best meet their goals for their students. It is recommended that students be formatively assessed on the thinking skills as this an ongoing process and all progress should be celebrated and acknowledged.

Time Allotment

Each lesson in this unit is intended to be taught in 60–90 minutes, but some lessons may take less or more time. In general, this unit can be taught in 15–20 hours of instructional time.

Unit Goals and Objectives

Concept

To develop conceptual awareness of divergent thinking skills using cross-curricular lessons, the students will:

- ❏ Develop an understanding of strategies used to generate many and varied ideas quickly
- ❏ Learn methods for applying flexibility of thought when changing points of view both visually and abstractly
- ❏ Discover how elaborating and adding details to art and writing can make a piece more interesting

❏ Discover how innovative thinking produces unique ideas and inventions
❏ Learn to set an intentional purpose when crafting solutions, considering both the purpose and audience for which the solution is intended

Process

To develop creative problem-solving skills based on divergent thinking strategies, the students will:

❏ Withhold judgments while generating ideas
❏ Learn to fluently generate many and varied ideas to develop the skill of flexible thinking
❏ Consider multiple perspectives, develop flexibility in thinking, and examine various viewing angles in exploring a variety of novel scenarios
❏ Work in cross-curricular contexts to develop ideas and solutions through elaboration
❏ Generate innovative, unique, and original ideas through collaboration and modification of existing ideas to create new and original products
❏ Work to refine ideas in purposeful, authentic contexts by exploring action plans, audiences, and limitations of solutions

Standards Alignment

Common Core State Standards (CCSS)

Standards are aligned with each of the five thinking skills targeted in the series *Integrated Lessons in Higher Order Thinking Skills*. Specific thinking skills are noted using the following key (see also Table P.2):

❏ A: Analytical Thinking
❏ C: Convergent Thinking
❏ D: Divergent Thinking
❏ E: Evaluative Thinking
❏ V: Visual-Spatial Thinking

NAGC Programming Standards Alignment

Teaching thinking skills aligns with NAGC programming standards as best practice for gifted students:

TABLE P.2
CCSS Alignment

Language Standards	CCR Anchor Standards for Reading *1, 6, 7, 8*	❏ Draw logical inferences from text (C/E) ❏ Cite text evidence to support claims (C/E) ❏ Assess perspectives (A/C/D/E/V) ❏ Evaluate various content formats (A/C/D/E/V) ❏ Evaluate arguments based on evidence (E)
	CCR Anchor Standards for Writing *1, 3, 4, 8, 9, 10*	❏ Write arguments, citing text evidence and using valid reasoning (C/E) ❏ Write narratives (D) ❏ Develop written work appropriate to a variety of tasks (A/C/D/E/V) ❏ Evaluate and synthesize information from a variety of sources (E) ❏ Draw evidence to support analysis (A) ❏ Write routinely and for many purposes (A/C/D/E/V)
	CCR Anchor Standards for Speaking and Listening *1, 2, 3, 4*	❏ Collaborate for a variety of purposes with a variety of partners (A/C/D/E/V) ❏ Integrate information from a variety of sources (A/C/D/E/V) ❏ Critically evaluate speakers' perspectives (E) ❏ Present information, including evidence, in ways that allow others to follow lines of reasoning (A/C/E)
	CCR Anchor Standards for Language *3, 5, 6*	❏ Make effective use of appropriate language in a variety of contexts (A/C/D/E/V) ❏ Understand and make use of figurative language (A/D/E) ❏ Develop and apply academic vocabulary (A/C/D/E/V)
Mathematics Standards	CCSS for Mathematics: Practice Standards	❏ Make sense of problems and persevere in solving them ❏ Reason abstractly and quantitatively ❏ Construct viable arguments and critique the reasoning of others ❏ Model with mathematics ❏ Use appropriate tools strategically ❏ Attend to precision ❏ Look for and make use of structure ❏ Look for and express regularity in repeated reasoning *Applicable to problems presented in all Thinking Skills units.*

(Continued)

TABLE P.2
(Continued)

	CCSS for Mathematics: Operations and Algebraic Thinking 2.OA, 3.OA, 4.OA, 5.OA	❑ Generate and analyze patterns and relationships (A/C/V) ❑ Represent problems both concretely and abstractly (A/C/V)
	CCSS for Mathematics: Measurement and Data 2.MD, 3.MD, 4.MD, 5.MD	❑ Represent and interpret data (A/C/V)
	CCSS for Mathematics: Geometry 2.G, 3.G, 4.G, 5.G	❑ Solve problems involving the coordinate plane (V) ❑ Solve problems involving lines, angles, and dimensions (V) ❑ Reason with shapes and their attributes (V)

- ❑ **Standard 1**: Students create awareness of and interest in their learning and cognitive growth
- ❑ **Standard 2**: Thinking skill aligned assessments provide evidence of learning progress
- ❑ **Standard 3**: Explicit instruction in thinking skills and metacognitive strategies is research-based best practice and meets the needs of gifted students for opportunities to develop depth, complexity, and abstraction in thinking and inquiry
- ❑ **Standard 5**: Competence in thinking skills promotes cognitive, social-emotional, and psychosocial development of students

Bibliography

Abrami, P.C., Bernard, R.M., Borokhovski, E., Wade, A., Surkes, M.A., Tamim, R., and Zhang, D. (2008). *Instructional interventions affecting critical thinking skills and dispositions: A stage 1 meta-analysis. Review of Educational Research, 78*(4), 1102–1134.

Common Core State Standards Initiative. (2022a). Common core state standards for English language arts & literacy in history/social studies, science, and technical subjects. http://www.corestandards.org/wp-content/uploads/ELA_Standards1.pdf.

Common Core State Standards Initiative. (2022b) Common core state standards for mathematics. http://www.corestandards.org/wp-content/uploads/Math_Standards1.pdf.

Dweck, C.S. (2006). *Mindset: The new psychology of success*. New York: Random House.

Eberle, B. (1996). *SCAMPER*. Waco, TX: Prufrock Press.

Gordon, W.J.J., and Pose, T. (1977). *The metaphorical way of learning and knowing*. Cambridge, MA: Porpoise Books.

Isaksen, S.G., Dorval, K.B., and Treffiner, D.J. (1998). *Toolbox for creative problem solving*. Williamsville, NY: Creative Problem Solving Group.

Kaplan, S. and Gould, B. (1995, 2003). *Depth & complexity icons, OERI, Javits project T.W.O. 2. Educator to educator. LVI.* J. Taylor Education, 2016.

NAGC Professional Standards Committee. (2018–2019). 2019 Pre-K-grade 12 gifted programming standards. https://www.nagc.org/sites/default/files/standards/Intro%202019%20Programming%20Standards.pdf

Osborn, A.F. (1953). *Applied imagination*. New York: Scribner.

Parnes, S.J. (9181). *The magic of your mind*. Buffalo, NY: Bearly Limited.

Treffinger, D.J., Isaksen, S.G., and Dorval, K.B. (2006). *Creative problem solving: An introduction* (4th ed.). Waco, TX: Prufrock.

Wagner, T., and Compton, R.A. (2012). *Creating innovators: The making of young people who will change the world*. New York: Scribner.

Introduction to Divergent Thinking

Materials

- ❏ Handout I.1: Divergent Thinking: Do It Like an Artist! (one per student)
- ❏ Handout I.2: Framing the Thinking of an Artist (one per student)
- ❏ Primary Source Artwork (enlarged either with a document camera or by copying in large format) Note: Online versions of the artwork with zoom-in features are available at
  - ■ https://www.artic.edu/artworks/111060/daniel-henry-kahnweiler
  - ■ https://www.georgesbraque.org/the-portuguese.jsp#prettyPhoto
- ❏ Handout I.3: About the Artists (one per student)
- ❏ Handout I.4: Primary Source Analysis: Artwork Analysis (one per small group of students)
- ❏ Handout I.5: Divergent Thinking Avatar (one per student)

Introduction: Frame of the Discipline

- ❏ Tell students they will be learning how to think using *divergent* reasoning. Creativity is a divergent thought process which involves generating new and unique possibilities in response to problems and challenges. The four cognitive skill areas utilized most in creative thinking are fluency, flexibility, originality, and elaboration.
- ❏ Read aloud the article Divergent Thinking: Do It Like an Artist! (Handout I.1).

DOI: 10.4324/9781003267959-1

❏ Model answering the questions on the page Framing the Thinking of an Artist (Handout I.2). See key understandings to target in Box I.1.

Box I.1: Framing the Thinking of an Artist Key Understandings

❏ *What questions do artists ask?*
  - I wonder…
  - What would happen if I…
  - How can I portray this idea differently?
  - How can I show my ideas through art?
❏ *What tools or thinking skills does an artist need?*
  - Able to observe and wonder about the world.
  - Able to come up with unique ideas.
  - Able to explore with different art mediums (paint, clay, weaving).
  - Look at the world from different perspectives.
❏ *Why are artists important in today's world?*
  - Artists offer unique perspectives on the world around us.
  - Artists make the world a more beautiful place.
  - Art is inspirational.
  - Art depicts what is happening in the world and serves as a historical reflection.
❏ *How do artists think about new information?*
  - Artists think critically about new information.
  - Artists ponder the meaning behind the new information.
  - Artists wonder how they can express the new information in a new and unique way.
❏ *Describe the main purpose of an artist.*
  - Artists enhance society by sharing their unique perspectives about the world through artistic expression.

Tell students that throughout this unit they will be thinking like an artist to generate new and unique possibilities in response to problems and challenges.

Handout I.1: Divergent Thinking: Do it Like an Artist

Name: _____

Creative thinking is the ability to view the world in new and unique ways and to take action based on that view. Creative thinkers are **imaginative, original,** and **flexible** in their thinking, allowing their ideas to blossom and form freely. Creative thinkers also collaborate with others. This sharing of ideas allows for **fluency,** or a greater number of ideas. As the ideas form, the creative mind looks for combinations and **elaborates** on the idea, adding details to create something new and unique.

Artists view the world through a variety of lenses and create art to depict the changes in our lives, in our communities, and in the world. Artists allow themselves to bounce around from idea to idea and then determine which option they would like to create a final product. Artists think creatively using their imaginations to generate new ideas. Then they must think critically to give purpose or value to the ideas they generate.

Artists prepare by **exploring the environment.** They think about the world and the various viewpoints of the people around them. Artists use the environment to spark new and creative ideas. Often artists jot down ideas in a notebook to further explore later. Artists may also do research at this stage, looking for additional information about the idea or works already created on this topic.

Next, artists **investigate ideas and materials.** Once an idea in the environment catches the artists interest they need to time to play around with the idea, make sketches, or try out a variety of paint brushes or art supplies to see what medium best expresses their idea.

Artists also **experiment with production** ideas. Artists manipulate and experiment with the various mediums and work to create a piece that depicts their new idea. It is helpful to understand that as ideas continue to develop, the product or piece of art may come to a close. Artists stop and revise or begin new art throughout this process.

Handout I.2: Framing the Thinking of an Artist

Name: _____

What questions do artists ask?	What tools or thinking skills does a artists need?

Describe the main purpose of an artists.

Why are artists important in today's world?	How do artists think about new information?

Primary Source: Artwork Analysis

❏ Prepare the artwork for display to students. In viewing the artwork, students will first view the paintings one at a time and then compare the paintings side by side. The images may be viewed either through projection via document camera or by printing an enlarged version from the link in the materials list.

❏ Tell students that Pablo Picasso and Georges Braque created a new art movement called cubism. The paintings they will be studying are done in the cubist style. These pieces depict Braque and Picasso's joint exploration using a new pictorial strategy for representing shapes in space. They looked at subjects in a unique way, trying to depict three-dimensional items on a flat canvas. The technique involved breaking up the subject into many shapes. They would then look at the shapes from a variety of angles. Finally, they would reconstruct the subject by painting the shapes from different angles. To build background knowledge about the art, read together or allow students time to read the information presented in Handout I.3, About the Art.

❏ Display Georges Braque's *The Portuguese*, 1911–1912. Direct students to look carefully at the painting and think about it like an artist. Invite students to use their senses, observe carefully, and think about what they may already know. If needed, guide students with question stems such as the following:
  ■ What do you notice about this painting?
  ■ What do you think the artist was trying to represent in the painting?
  ■ What questions do you have?
  ■ What can you tell about the subject of the painting?
  ■ What else do you still wonder?

❏ Display Pablo Picasso's *Daniel-Henry Kahnweiler*, 1910. Invite students to again use their senses, observe carefully, and ask some questions about the painting. Use the same questions to guide the discussion.

❏ Provide students with Handout I.4: Primary Source: Artwork Analysis. Remind students of the information they have read about cubism (Handout I.3) and invite them to look at both paintings side by side. Discuss the entirety of the paintings, using questions such as:
  ■ What do you notice when looking at the paintings side by side?
  ■ What are your feelings about the painting?
  ■ What conclusions can you draw?

❏ Give students the Primary Source: Artwork Analysis page (Handout I.4). Guide students through answering each section on the page. Remind

Handout I.3: About the Art

Name: _____

Cubism was a new art movement created by Georges Braque and Pablo Picasso. Braque and Picasso painted abstractly, leaving few signs of the real world in their paintings. They looked at subjects in a unique way, trying to depict three-dimensional items on a two-dimensional flat canvas. The technique involved breaking up the subject into many shapes. They would then look at the shapes from a variety of angles. Finally, the they would reconstruct the subject by painting the shapes from different angles. This style of art aims to show all the possible viewpoints of the object at the same time in one painting.

It was named cubism because the artwork looked like it was recreated using cubes and geometric shapes. Cubists used geometric shapes such as cones, cylinders, and spheres to represent the natural world. The paintings represented distorted and deformed figures from the natural world which may or may not include the whole figure Cubism challenged perspective and explored space on the canvas through blending the foreground and background.

The use of multiple perspectives allowed the artists to draw the subjects with greater truth and accuracy. For example, when drawing an item using visual perspectives, the true shape of the item is distorted.

During the initial development of cubism, Braque and Picasso used muted colors that were monochromatic, meaning various shades of the same color. This was done so that the viewer would not be distracted by the colors and would pay close attention to the shapes and forms depicted. Then in 1912, Picasso began to explore painting with colors and invented the collage technique. He experimented with pasting pieces of colorful paper onto their paintings.

While both artists co-created these techniques, Picasso is often considered to be more famous and critically acclaimed. However, both Braque and Picasso contributed to making the cubist movement.

Based on information from pablopicasso.org and georgesbraque.org

Handout I.4: Primary Source: Artwork

Name: _____

The Portuguése by Georges Braque, 1911-1912	*Daniel-Henry Kahnweiler,* By Pablo Picasso, 1910

FACTS
- What do we know about this painting?
- What type of painting is this?
- Who painted it?
- When was it created?
- What does it depict?

CUBISM
Explain cubism using these words: shape, color, line, perspective, and angles.

CREATIVITY
How did these artist show creativity? Originality? Flexibility of thought?

❏ students that primary sources offer genuine insights into how artists use creative thinking. Key understandings from the artwork analysis are outlined in Box I.2.

❏ Remind students they are using divergent thinking when analyzing these paintings.

Box I.2: Primary Source: Artwork Analysis Key Understandings

❏ *Facts about* The Portuguese.
  ■ Painted by Georges Braque, 1911
  ■ Painted using the early cubist style
  ■ Portraying a guitar player and a dock
❏ *Facts about* Daniel-Henry Kahnweiler.
  ■ Painted by Pablo Picasso, 1910
  ■ Painted using the early cubism style
  ■ Portrait of Daniel-Henry Kahnweiler
❏ *Explain cubism.*
  ■ Cubism is an abstract form of painting in which the subjects are broken into many shapes. Then the artist looks at the shapes from a variety of perspectives and angles. Finally, the subject is recreated using the fractured shapes in muted monochromatic colors so that the viewer focuses on the shapes and forms. Cubism challenged perspective and explored space on the canvas by blending the foreground and background.
❏ *How did the artists show creativity?*
  ■ The artists showed creativity by flexibly breaking subjects into fragments and then putting them back together in a unique and original format.

Thinking Skills Avatar

❏ The final introductory lesson involves students creating their own Divergent Thinking Avatar. Today, students will decorate their Avatar. Distribute Handout I.5.

Handout I.5: Divergent Thinking Avatar

Name: _____

CREATE YOUR DIVERGENT THINKING AVATAR.

GENERATE IDEAS LIKE:

CHANGE PERSPECTIVES LIKE:

AM INNOVATIVE LIKE:

ELABORATE ON IDEAS LIKE:

GIVE IDEAS PURPOSE LIKE:

❏ Discuss with students the concept of an avatar. An avatar is a symbolic representation of a person that can be used as a stand-in. As you move through the divergent thinking sub-skills in this unit, this page will serve as a touch point for students to connect the skills together into one representation of divergent thinking.

❏ Explain that throughout this unit they will be introduced to five learning targets:
  ■ Generating Ideas
  ■ Changing Perspectives
  ■ Elaborating
  ■ Innovating
  ■ Giving Ideas Purpose

❏ As students complete each target learning skill, they will pause and reflect on the key details of each sub-skill. Use the sub-skill boxes to record the keys ideas and/or illustrate a new avatar using the newly learned skill. This is a time for the students to synthesize their learning.

❏ For today, allow students time to illustrate their avatar (the outline in the top left box) to represent a divergent thinking character/avatar of their choice. The other five boxes will remain empty for now, being filled in as students complete each sub-skill in the unit.

Bibliography

Braque, G. (1911). *The Portuguese [painting]*. Basel, Switzerland: Basel Kunstmuseum. https://www.georgesbraque.org/the-portuguese.jsp#prettyPhoto.

Georges Braque Biography. (2009). https://georgesbraque.org/georges-braque-biography.jsp

Pablo Picasso Biography. (n.d.). https://pablopicasso.org/picasso-biography.jsp.

Picasso, P. (1910). *Daniel-Henry Kahnweiler [painting]*. Chicago, IL: Chicago Art Institute. https://www.artic.edu/artworks/111060/daniel-henry-kahnweiler.

CHAPTER 1

Sub-Skill 1

Generating Ideas

TABLE 1.1
Generating Ideas Sub-Skills Overview

Thinking Skill Outline	
Focus Questions	❑ How many ideas can I think of? ❑ How **fluently** can I generate ideas?
Lesson 1	*Avoiding Judgment* ❑ **Trade Book Focus:** *The Happy Dreamer* by Peter Reynolds ❑ **Practice Activity:** Students will brainstorm ways to stop a dog from running away every time the door is opened.
Lesson 2	*Developing Fluency* ❑ **Trade Book Focus:** *Round Trip* by Ann Jonas ❑ **Practice Activity:** Students will brain-write ideas for the situation: "Ugh! It's raining again! That means no outdoor recess. How can our class get exercise and have some fun during our recess time?"
Authentic Application Activity	*Force-Fitting Ideas Together* ❑ **Story Focus:** Cinderella ❑ **Practice Activity:** Students will use force-fitting to force current inventions into the story of Cinderella and see the new story possibilities.

DOI: 10.4324/9781003267959-2

Generating Ideas Lesson 1:
Avoiding Judgment

Objective: Generate many and varied ideas quickly while withholding judgment.

Materials

- ❏ Handout 1.1 Generating Ideas Anchor Chart (one enlarged copy for the class)
- ❏ Everyday items (pencil, plastic fork, eggbeater, etc.)
- ❏ Handout 1.2: What is Generating? (one per student)
- ❏ *The Happy Dreamer* by Peter Reynolds (teacher's copy)
- ❏ Handout 1.3: Creating Thinking Guidelines Anchor Chart (one enlarged copy for the class)
- ❏ Handout 1.4: Read Aloud Reflection (one per student)
- ❏ Handout 1.5: Brainstorming (one per student)

Whole Group Introduction

- ❏ Tell students that we will be discussing the thinking skill of fluency or generating many ideas.
- ❏ Share the Generating Ideas Anchor Chart (Handout 1.1). Tell students that generating ideas fluently is the ability to produce many ideas, or possibilities. Fluent thinkers withhold judgment and brainstorm large quantities of ideas.
- ❏ Choose an everyday object like a pencil, plastic fork, or eggbeater. Pass the object around, asking students to produce a new use for the object. For example, a plastic fork could be a hair comb, a pitchfork for a mouse, a sling shot, etc. Encourage students to bounce ideas off one another and piggyback on each other's ideas. Continue this game for a couple of items, trying to ensure that each student is given the opportunity to generate an idea. You may need to prompt students to get their creative juices flowing. Remind students that when thinking creatively, there aren't any bad ideas—even silly ideas are welcome.

GENERATING IDEAS

FLUENTLY THINKING OF AS MANY IDEAS AS POSSIBLE

❏ Point out to students that the game they just played encourages generating ideas and fluent thinking. Tell the students that today they will be using their imagination to think fluently and generate many ideas.

❏ A vocabulary lesson is provided for students to learn the different forms of the word *generate*. In this unit the various forms of the word will be used, and this lesson will build schema before students are expected to apply the word.

❏ Distribute What is Generating? (Handout 1.2). Explain that the word *generate* is both a verb and a noun depending upon the suffix added to the base word. Remind students:

  ■ a noun is a person, place, thing, or idea
  ■ a verb is an action

❏ Tell students that as a verb, generate means to create new ideas, or to produce something, like electricity. When we change the form of the word to *generation*, it becomes a noun and can mean two things: 1) a stage of improvement on an invention or idea or 2) a group of people born at a certain time, like Generation Z.

❏ Read the definitions and sentence with the students. Discuss the sentences and decide which form of the word fits. Discuss how the word becomes a different form depending on how it is used in a sentence.

❏ Direct students to cut out the words at the bottom, determine which form of the word fits each definition and sentence, and then place the word under the sentence. Circulate to check for understanding before allowing students to glue down their answers.

Read Aloud Activity

Teacher's note: Fluency is the ability to produce a large number of ideas, or possibilities. Fluent thinkers withhold judgment and brainstorm large quantities of ideas. Fluent thinking promotes the idea that having a larger number of ideas to choose from will often result in a greater probability of having a quality idea. Examples of questions which encourage fluent thinking are:

❏ In what ways might we…?
❏ How might we…?
❏ How many ways can you think to…?
❏ Make a list of at least 40 ideas for…
❏ How many examples of _____ can you think of?

❏ Tell students you will be reading a book in which the character uses fluent thinking. Read the book *The Happy Dreamer* by Peter H. Reynolds. This book invites the reader on a journey with a little boy who is a

Handout 1.2: What is GENERATING?

Name: _____

Created new ideas

Thomas Edison _____ many new ideas.

verb (past)

To create new ideas

_____ new ideas comes easily to me.

verb

To produce

The solar panels _____ electricity.

verb

A stage in improving a past product

This is the new and improved iPhone _____.

noun

| generated | generate | generating | generation |

dreamer, reminding us there are many paths to follow and many ways to be a dreamer. Ask students how this book shows fluent thinking.

❏ Distribute the Read Aloud Reflection page (Handout 1.4).

❏ Direct students to carefully consider and answer the questions on the top half. When students have finished, discuss responses as a whole group. Key understandings for the read aloud are outlined in Box 1.1.

❏ Before going on to the next section of the page, introduce the Creative Thinking Guidelines poster (Handout 1.3) to the students. Explain that throughout this unit, it is important to follow these guidelines. Discuss what each rule means.

■ **Avoid judging the ideas:** Allow ideas to just be ideas; they are not good ideas or bad ideas. If we qualify the idea, then the rest of the thinking is stunted.

■ **Generate *many* ideas:** Strive to generate many ideas, and push past the first few obvious ideas. Often the best ideas are thought of after letting our brains loosen up and freewheel.

■ **Stretch your mind:** Try to generate unique, off-the-wall, or zany ideas.

■ **Combine and connect ideas:** Work to bounce ideas off one another, and allow piggybacking on each other's ideas. Push two seemingly different ideas together and see what happens.

❏ After the brief discussion, have students write the guidelines in their own words, and then create an image or symbol to represent each rule.

Box 1.1: *The Happy Dreamer* Key Understandings

❏ Summarize the main idea of *The Happy Dreamer*.
■ The boy is a dreamer. He dreams happily, quietly, loudly, and colorfully. At times he feels boxed in and sad, but he always bounces back and begins to dream again. He is a creative, happy, dreamer.

❏ How did the author show fluency?
■ This book shows how the boy is fluently dreaming in multiple ways. He tries to dream in as many ways as possible.

❏ Generating Rules—In my own words:
■ *Don't judge* the ideas as good or bad.
■ Create *lots* of ideas.
■ Look for *novel ideas* which are silly, wild, or strange.
■ *Piggyback* on someone else's idea.

CREATIVE THINKING
Guidelines

1. Avoid Judging the Ideas
If we judge the ideas too soon the thinking is stunted.

2. Generate MANY Ideas
Strive to generate multiple ideas
and push beyond the obvious ideas.

3. Stretch your Mind
Look for new or unique ideas

4. Combine and Connect Ideas
Bounce ideas off one another,
and piggyback on other's ideas

Skill Development Activity

❏ Explain that **brainstorming** is a useful tool when you have an open-ended task in need of many or unique options. Tell students that today they will use both quiet brainstorming and oral brainstorming to create a list of ideas to solve a problem.

❏ Distribute the Brainstorming page (Handout 1.4). Read aloud: Doggonit! Every time the door is opened your dog runs out of the house. He loves to "take himself" on a walk but in the process, he comes back inside covered in mud. You go out to do some investigating and notice there is a mud puddle in the neighbor's yard. Both of your parents are upset about the dog's behavior. What's a kid to do? In the next 5 minutes, silently brainstorm a list of ways to solve the problem: How could you get your dog to stop running away and getting dirty?

❏ Allow students independent, silent time (5–10 minutes) to generate as many ideas as possible and record them on this page.

❏ After the time limit is up, students will call out their ideas while a recorder captures all the ideas on a large piece of chart paper.

❏ Use encouraging prompts to further the brainstorming, such as, "Let's keep thinking of more ideas," or "What else can you think of that no one else has said?"

❏ Try to push through the obvious first 15–20 responses. Encourage students to aim for 50 ideas. Close the activity when all ideas have been generated. *Teacher tip*: Wait time is powerful here!

Generating Ideas Lesson 2: Developing Fluency

Objective: Generate many and varied ideas quickly.

Materials

❏ More everyday items (pencil, plastic fork, eggbeater, etc.)
❏ *Round Trip* by Ann Jonas (teacher's copy)
❏ Handout 1.6: Read Aloud Reflection (one per student)
❏ Handout 1.7: Brain-writing (one per student)

Handout 1.4: Read Aloud Reflection
The Happy Dreamer by Peter H. Reynolds.

Name: _____

Summarize the main idea of *The Happy Dreamer*?	How did the author show fluency?

Generating Rule: Producing MANY new ideas.	**In my own words.**	**Symbol**
Don't judge the ideas as good or bad.		
Create LOTS of ideas		
Look for **novel ideas** which are silly, wild, or strange.		
Piggyback on someone else's idea.		

Handout 1.5: Brainstorming

Name: _____

Doggonit! Every time someone opens the door your dog runs out of the house. He loves to "take himself" on a walk but in the process, he comes back in covered in mud. You go out to do some investigating and notice there is a mud puddle in the neighbor's yard. Both of your parents are upset about the dog's behavior. What's a kid to do? In the next 5 minutes, silently brainstorm a list of ways to solve the problem: How could you get your dog to stop running away and getting dirty?

Share out your ideas, as someone records all the ideas on a piece of chart paper.

Whole Group Introduction

- ❏ Remind students that in their last lesson, they discovered that fluent thinkers generate many and varied ideas while withholding judgment.
- ❏ Review the Generating Ideas Anchor Chart with students. Tell students that when generating ideas, they must also think fluently, or quickly, and flexibly. Flexible thinking means they must look at things differently and come up with new or unique ideas. Often flexible thinking occurs when forcing two seemingly different ideas together to find a new solution.
- ❏ Tell students you are going to play a game called Connection. In this game, the teacher will select two random ideas or items and ask students to think "How is _____ like a _____?" Students are forced to make a connection between the words. Encourage students to come up with as many connections between the items as possible. For example:
  - How is a pencil like a plastic fork? (They are both tools you use with your hands.)
  - How is a flower like a dog? (They are both alive. They both grow.)
  - Continue asking the students to make connections and encouraging outside-of-the-box thinking.
- ❏ Tell the students that by playing the game of Connection they used their imaginations to think fluently and flexibly.

Read Aloud Activity

- ❏ Tell students you will be reading a book in which the author uses fluent and flexible thinking. Read the book *Round Trip* by Ann Jonas. This book has black-and-white illustrations and text which detail a day trip to the city and back home again. The trip to the city is read front to back and the trip home is read back to front when the book is flipped upside down. After reading, ask students: How did the author show creative thinking when creating this book?
- ❏ Distribute the Read Aloud Reflection page (Handout 1.6). Direct students to carefully consider and answer the questions on the top half. When students have finished, discuss responses as a whole group. Key understandings for the read aloud are outlined in Box 1.2.
- ❏ Tell students that in the bottom half of the paper they will be writing a synectics sentence. Explain that creating synectics sentences is similar to playing the game Connection. Synectics is joining ideas through connections and encourages students to think through metaphors or

Handout 1.6: Read Aloud Reflection
Round Trip by Ann Jonas

Name: _____

How did the author show flexible thinking?

What do you see below? Is there more than one animal here?
HINT: Rotate the paper.

Try drawing your own version.

Anynomous Illustrator, 1892. 'Welche Thiere gleichen einander am meisten?' Fliegende Blätter. Braun & Schneider.

Using the information from the text, pick one of the items, (or an item of your choice) and complete these statements:

A drive to the city is like a(n)_____ because_____
_____
_____

A drive to the country is like a(n) _____ because_____
_____
_____

analogies about the content. Two concepts or objects are compared and related through forced comparison and analogy. For example: "My baby brother is like a kazoo because they are both annoyingly loud."

❑ Model completing the synectics sentence. Write on the board, "A drive to the beach is like a _____ because_____."
Allow students to look at the pictures on their handout, then model thinking out loud, "Out of these options I like the magnet. Hmm what do magnets do? They repel (push) or attract (pull). What about: A drive to the beach is like a magnet because I feel the water pulling me closer."

❑ Remind students there are no right or wrong answers. This is an opportunity to be creative and look for a variety of connections.

Box 1.2: *Round Trip* Key Understandings

❑ This book is a round trip of a story. The author showed flexible thinking by drawing a story in black and white in which the pictures tell a story both forward and backward. The trip to the city is read front to back and the trip home is read back to front when the book is flipped upside down. This is an inventive book with amazing creativity and a unique look at perspective.

Skill Development Activity

❑ Tell students that brain-writing is a quieter form of brainstorming where all students write their ideas on a sheet of paper; after a time limit, the papers are passed to the next person. Students then add to the ideas of their peers. This helps with students who need quiet think time to generate ideas.

❑ Seat group members at a table and give each person Handout 1.7. Read aloud the directions: "Ugh! It's raining again! That means no outdoor recess. How can our class get exercise and have some fun during our recess time?"

❑ Give the students 3 minutes to write down three ideas for how to solve the problem on their paper. Allow students to write in "free form." Do not permit any discussion.

❑ After 3 minutes, have students pass their papers to the right so that everyone has a new paper. Ask students to read the previous ideas and add three more ideas to the list. The new ideas may be completely new or piggyback off the other person's ideas. Continue in this fashion until you think you have enough ideas—roughly 5–10 rounds.

Name: _____

Ugh! It's raining again! That means no outdoor recess. How can our class get exercise and have some fun during our recess time? In the next three minutes, write down at least three ideas for how to solve the problem. When I call time, pass your paper to the right, read the previous ideas and add three more ideas to the list. Remember the new ideas may be completely new or piggyback off the other person's ideas.

When you get your paper back, review all the ideas on your paper.
We will share out the ideas to create a class list.

❏ When the rounds are complete, collect the papers and record all the ideas on a large sheet of paper for everyone to see. (Or allow students to call out their ideas as a recorder writes the options on chart paper, creating a class list.)

❏ Discuss which ideas would work best for solving the current problem.

Generating Ideas Authentic Application Activity: Force-Fitting Ideas Together

Objective: Apply the skill of fluency to generate many and varied ideas to solve a problem.

Materials

❏ Handout 1.8: The Cinderella Story (one story per student, project the story, or do a read aloud)

❏ Handout 1.9: Force-Fitting (one per student)

Authentic Application

❏ Review the Generating Ideas Anchor Chart. Remind students that when they generate ideas, they need to think fluently and flexibly. Creative thinkers withhold judgment and generate large quantities of ideas.

❏ Distribute the Cinderella story to the class (Handout 1.8) or display it in a way that all students can see the text. Tell students to highlight the problems Cinderella faces as you read the story together (or model highlighting on the class copy).

❏ Discuss the problems in the story:
  ■ The step-sisters are mean.
  ■ Cinderella does all the work.
  ■ She must get back and forth to the ball before her riches turn into rags.
  ■ Cinderella loses the glass slipper.

❏ Distribute the Force-Fitting page (Handout 1.9). Tell students that force-fitting involves using unrelated items and forcing them together to create a new or unusual option for solving a problem. It involves forcing together two dissimilar, or unrelated, objects or ideas to generate a

TABLE 1.2
Force-Fitting Cinderella Examples

Item	When in the story?	How could it help?
bike	when running out of the palace	She could use it to get home before midnight.
cell phone	when the clock struck midnight	Cinderella could use the cell phone to call the Fairy Godmother and ask to stay a little later.
computer	when she needed a dress	She could order a dress for the ball.

new possibility. Explain that force-fitting helps to find new and unique ways to use everyday objects or ideas in an unusual manner.

❏ Instruct students to look at the pictures. Tell students to think:

  ■ When in the story might Cinderella have used a bike? Allow students time to discuss and share out their ideas.

  ■ How might these items serve Cinderella? Allow students time to discuss and share out their ideas.

  ■ Continue asking *when* and *how* questions in this manner for the cell phone and computer. Encourage students to think creatively and outside the box.

❏ Optional Extension: Have students re-write the story adding one invention. How will the addition of an invention change the story?

Generating Ideas Concluding Activities

❏ Distribute the Generating Ideas Exit Ticket (Appendix A). Ask students to reflect on their learning about the skill of generating ideas. Allow time for students to complete the exit ticket. Use this as a formative assessment, to gain a better understanding of your students' readiness to effectively practice the skill of generating ideas.

❏ If desired, complete the Group Observation Rubric (Appendix A) to track students' progress with the skill.

❏ Ask students to retrieve their Divergent Thinking Avatar (Handout I.5). In the Generating Ideas box, they should either write the main ideas about the thinking skill or illustrate their avatar using the skill of generating ideas.

Handout 1.8: *Cinderella*

Name: _____

Once there was a gentleman who married, for his second wife, the proudest and most haughty woman that was ever seen. She had, by a former husband, two daughters of her own, who were, indeed, exactly like her in all things. He had likewise, by another wife, a young daughter, but of unparalleled goodness and sweetness of temper, which she took from her mother, who was the best creature in the world.

No sooner were the ceremonies of the wedding over, but the stepmother began to show herself in her true colors. She could not bear the good qualities of this pretty girl, and the less because they made her own daughters appear the more odious. She employed her in the meanest work of the house. She scoured the dishes, tables, etc., and cleaned madam's chamber, and those of misses, her daughters. She slept in a sorry garret, on a wretched straw bed, while her sisters slept in fine rooms, with floors all inlaid, on beds of the very newest fashion, and where they had looking glasses so large that they could see themselves at their full length from head to foot.

The poor girl bore it all patiently, and dared not tell her father, who would have scolded her for his wife governed him entirely. When she had done her work, she used to go to the chimney corner, and sit down there in the cinders and ashes, which caused her to be called Cinderwench. Only the younger sister, who was not as rude and uncivil as the older one, called her Cinderella. However, Cinderella, notwithstanding her coarse apparel, was a hundred times more beautiful than her sisters, although they were always dressed very richly.

It happened that the king's son gave a ball and invited all persons of fashion to it. Our young misses were also invited, for they cut a very grand figure among those of quality. They were mightily delighted at this invitation, and wonderfully busy in selecting the gowns, petticoats, and hair dressing that would best become them. This was a new difficulty for Cinderella for it was she who ironed her sister's linen and pleated their ruffles. They talked all day long of nothing but how they should be dressed.

"For my part," said the eldest, "I will wear my red velvet suit with French trimming."

"And I," said the youngest, "shall have my usual petticoat; but then, to make amends for that, I will put on my gold-flowered cloak, and my diamond stomacher, which is far from being the most ordinary one in the world."

They sent for the best hairdresser they could get to make up their headpieces and adjust their hairdos, and they had their red brushes and patches from Mademoiselle de la Poche.

They also consulted Cinderella in all these matters, for she had excellent ideas, and her advice was always good. Indeed, she even offered her services to fix their hair, which they very willingly accepted. As she was doing this, they said to her, "Cinderella, would you not like to go to the ball?"

"Alas!" said she, "you only jeer me; it is not for such as I am to go to such a place."

1

"You are quite right," they replied. "It would make the people laugh to see a Cinderwench at a ball."

Anyone but Cinderella would have fixed their hair awry, but she was very good, and dressed them perfectly well. They were so excited that they hadn't eaten a thing for almost two days. Then they broke more than a dozen laces trying to have themselves laced up tightly enough to give them a fine slender shape. They were continually in front of their looking glass. At last, the happy day came. They went to court, and Cinderella followed them with her eyes as long as she could. When she lost sight of them, she started to cry.

Her godmother, who saw her all-in tears, asked her what was the matter.

"I wish I could. I wish I could." She was not able to speak the rest, being interrupted by her tears and sobbing.

This godmother of hers, who was a fairy, said to her, "You wish that you could go to the ball; is it not so?"

"Yes," cried Cinderella, with a great sigh.

"Well," said her godmother, "be but a good girl, and I will contrive that you shall go." Then she took her into her chamber, and said to her, "Run into the garden, and bring me a pumpkin."

Cinderella went immediately to gather the finest she could get, and brought it to her godmother, not being able to imagine how this pumpkin could help her go to the ball. Her godmother scooped out all the inside of it, leaving nothing but the rind. Having done this, she struck the pumpkin with her wand, and it was instantly turned into a fine coach, gilded all over with gold.

She then went to look into her mousetrap, where she found six mice, all alive, and ordered Cinderella to lift up a little the trapdoor. She gave each mouse, as it went out, a little tap with her wand, and the mouse was that moment turned into a fine horse, which altogether made a very fine set of six horses of a beautiful mouse colored dapple gray.

Being at a loss for a coachman, Cinderella said, "I will go and see if there is not a rat in the rat trap that we can turn into a coachman."

"You are right," replied her godmother, "Go and look."

Cinderella brought the trap to her, and in it, there were three huge rats. The fairy chose the one, which had the largest beard, touched him with her wand, and turned him into a fat, jolly coachman, who had the smartest whiskers that eyes ever beheld.

Handout 1.8, continued: *Cinderella*

After that, she said to her, "Go again into the garden, and you will find six lizards behind the watering pot. Bring them to me."

She had no sooner done so but her godmother turned them into six footmen, who skipped up immediately behind the coach, with their liveries all bedaubed with gold and silver, and clung as close behind each other as if they had done nothing else their whole lives. The fairy then said to Cinderella, "Well, you see here an equipage fit to go to the ball with; are you not pleased with it?"

"Oh, yes," she cried; "but must I go in these nasty rags?"

Her godmother then touched her with her wand, and, at the same instant, her clothes turned into cloth of gold and silver, all beset with jewels. This done, she gave her a pair of glass slippers, the prettiest in the whole world. Being thus decked out, she got up into her coach; but her godmother, above all things, commanded her not to stay past midnight, telling her, at the same time, that if she stayed one moment longer, the coach would be a pumpkin again, her horses mice, her coachman a rat, her footmen lizards, and that her clothes would become just as they were before.

She promised her godmother to leave the ball before midnight; and then drove away, scarcely able to contain herself for joy. The king's son, who was told that a great princess, whom nobody knew, had arrived, ran out to receive her. He gave her his hand as she alighted from the coach, and led her into the hall, among all the company. There was immediately a profound silence. Everyone stopped dancing, and the violins ceased to play, so entranced was everyone with the singular beauties of the unknown newcomer.

Nothing was then heard but a confused noise of, "How beautiful she is! How beautiful she is!"

The king himself, old as he was, could not help watching her, and telling the queen softly that it was a long time since he had seen such a beautiful and lovely a creature.

All the ladies were busied in considering her clothes and headdress, hoping to have some made the next day after the same pattern, provided they could find such fine materials and as able hands to make them.

The king's son led her to the most honorable seat, and afterwards took her out to dance with him. She danced so very gracefully that they all more and more admired her. A fine meal was served up, but the young prince ate not a morsel, so intently was he busied in gazing on her.

She went and sat down by her sisters, showing them a thousand civilities, giving them part of the oranges and citrons, which the prince had presented her with, which very much surprised them, for they did not know her. While Cinderella was thus amusing her sisters, she heard the clock strike eleven and three-quarters, whereupon she immediately made a courtesy to the company and hurried away as fast as she could.

Arriving home, she ran to seek out her godmother, and, after having thanked her, she said she could not but heartily wish she might go to the ball the next day as well, because the king's son had invited her.

As she was eagerly telling her godmother everything that had happened at the ball, her two sisters knocked at the door, which Cinderella ran and opened.

"You stayed such a long time!" she cried, gaping, rubbing her eyes and stretching herself as if she had been sleeping; she had not, however, had any manner of inclination to sleep while they were away from home.

"If you had been at the ball," said one of her sisters, "you would not have been tired with it. The finest princess was there, the most beautiful that mortal eyes have ever seen. She showed us a thousand civilities and gave us oranges and citrons."

Cinderella seemed very indifferent in the matter. Indeed, she asked them the name of that princess; but they told her they did not know it and that the king's son was very uneasy on her account and would give all the world to know who she was. At this Cinderella, smiling, replied, "She must, then, be very beautiful indeed; how happy you have been! Could not I see her? Ah, dear Charlotte, do lend me your yellow dress which you wear every day."

"Yes, to be sure!" cried Charlotte, "Lend my clothes to such a dirty Cinderwench as you are! I should be such a fool."

Cinderella, indeed, well expected such an answer, and was very glad of the refusal for she would have been sadly put to it, if her sister had lent her what she asked for jestingly.

The next day the two sisters were at the ball, and so was Cinderella, but dressed even more magnificently than before. The king's son was always by her, and never ceased his compliments and kind speeches to her. All this was so far from being tiresome to her, and, indeed, she quite forgot what her godmother had told her. She thought that it was no later than eleven when she counted the clock striking twelve. She jumped up and fled, as nimble as a deer. The prince followed but could not overtake her. She left behind one of her glass slippers, which the prince picked up most carefully. She reached home, but quite out of breath, and in her nasty old clothes, having nothing left of all her finery but one of the little slippers, the mate to the one that she had dropped.

The guards at the palace gate were asked if they had not seen a princess go out. They replied that they had seen nobody leave but a young girl, very shabbily dressed, and who had more the air of a poor country wench than a gentlewoman.

4

When the two sisters returned from the ball Cinderella asked them if they had been well entertained, and if the fine lady had been there.

They told her, yes, but that she hurried away immediately when it struck twelve, and with so much haste that she dropped one of her little glass slippers, the prettiest in the world, which the king's son had picked up; that he had done nothing but look at her all the time at the ball, and that most certainly he was very much in love with the beautiful person who owned the glass slipper.

What they said was very true; for a few days later, the king's son had it proclaimed, by sound of trumpet that he would marry her whose foot this slipper would just fit. They began to try it on the princesses, then the duchesses and all the court, but in vain; it was brought to the two sisters, who did all they possibly could to force their foot into the slipper, but they did not succeed.

Cinderella, who saw all this, and knew that it was her slipper, said to them, laughing, "Let me see if it will not fit me."

Her sisters burst out laughing and began to banter with her. The gentleman, who was sent to try the slipper looked earnestly at Cinderella, and, finding her very handsome, said that it was only just that she should try as well, and that he had orders to let everyone try.

He had Cinderella sit down, and, putting the slipper to her foot, he found that it went on very easily; fitting her as if it had been made of wax. Her two sisters were greatly astonished, but then even more so, when Cinderella pulled out of her pocket the other slipper and put it on her other foot. Then in came her godmother and touched her wand to Cinderella's clothes, making them richer and more magnificent than any of those she had worn before.

And now her two sisters found her to be that fine, beautiful lady whom they had seen at the ball. They threw themselves at her feet to beg pardon for all the ill treatment they had made her undergo. Cinderella took them up, and, as she embraced them, said that she forgave them with all her heart, and wanted them always to love her.

She was taken to the young prince, dressed as she was. He thought she was more charming than before, and, a few days after, married her. Cinderella, who was no less good than beautiful, gave her two sisters lodgings in the palace, and that very same day matched them with two great lords of the court.

Handout 1.9: Force-Fitting Cinderella

Name: _____

After reading the story, think about the problems that *Cinderella* faced in in the story. Help bring Cinderella into the 21st Century by adding a current invention to the story. Look at the pictures below. When in the story could this item have helped? How might these items serve Cinderella? Be sure to fully explain your ideas.

Item	When in the story could this item help?	How could this idea help Cinderella?
Your choice:		

Option: Rewrite the story adding a 21st Century invention. Be sure to include how this invention would change the story.

Bibliography

Anonymous Illustrator (1892). The Duck-Rabbit ambiguous figure. "Welche Thiere gleichen einander am meisten?" In *Fliegende Blätter*. Germany: Braun & Schneider.

Isaksen, S.G., Dorval, K.B., and Treffiner, D.J. (1998). *Toolbox for creative problem solving*. Williamsville, NY: Creative Problem Solving Group.

Jonas, A. (1983). *Round trip*. New York: Greenwillow.

Osborn, A.F. (1953). *Applied imagination*. New York: Scribner.

Parnes, S.J. (1981). *The magic of your mind*. Buffalo, NY: Bearly Limited.

Reynolds, P. (2017). *The happy dreamer*. New York: Scholastic Inc.

Treffinger, D.J., Isaksen, S.G., and Dorval, K.B. (2006). *Creative problem solving: An introduction* (4th ed.). Waco, TX: Prufrock.

CHAPTER 2

Sub-Skill 2

Changing Perspectives

TABLE 2.1
Changing Perspectives Sub-Skill Overview

Thinking Skill Outline	
Focus Questions	❏ What's another way of looking at this? ❏ How can I be **flexible** in my thinking? ❏ What else could we use this for? ❏ What relationship can you think of between _____ and _____?
Lesson 1	*Looking at Different Visual Perspectives* ❏ **Trade Book Focus:** *The Turn About, Think About, Look About Book* by Beau Gardner ❏ **Practice Activity:** Students rotate an image and create captions for each new viewpoint.
Lesson 2	*Understanding Others' Points of View* ❏ **Trade Book Focus:** *The Day the Crayons Quit* by Drew Daywalt ❏ **Practice Activity:** Students will do a gallery walk, looking at pictures from a variety of perspectives.
Authentic Application Activity	*Circle of Viewpoints* ❏ **Story Focus:** *Jack and the Beanstalk* ❏ **Practice Activity:** Circle of Viewpoints

DOI: 10.4324/9781003267959-3

Changing Perspectives Lesson 1: Looking at Different Visual Perspectives

Objective: Apply flexibility of thought when changing visual viewpoints.

Materials

- ❏ Handout 2.1: Changing Perspectives Anchor Chart (one enlarged copy for the class)
- ❏ *The Turn About, Think About, Look About Book* by Beau Gardner (teacher's copy)
- ❏ Handout 2.2: Read Aloud Reflection (one per student)
- ❏ Handouts 2.3.a–d: Varying Perspectives pages (duplicated as needed)

Whole Group Introduction

- ❏ Using the pairs of options listed here, ask students one question at a time, "What would you rather be? And why?" Allow students to share out with a shoulder partner or whole group. Make sure to include the why they chose their answer. Discuss the various reasons.
  - ■ A computer or a cell phone?
  - ■ A house or a school?
  - ■ A tree or a lake?
- ❏ Tell students they were just using flexible thinking when they played "What would you rather be?" In the game, they had to think about each item and, based on their perspective, choose the one they'd like to be.
- ❏ Introduce the creative thinking skill Changing Perspectives Anchor Chart. Explain to students that changing perspectives is the ability to flexibly look at things from a variety of viewpoints and angles, or to shift one's train of thought to produce a variety of ideas. Often flexible thinking occurs when forcing two seemingly different ideas together or when constraints prevent production of a simple solution.
- ❏ Tell the students that today they will be using their imagination to think fluently and flexibly.

CHANGING PERSPECTIVES

FLEXIBLY THINKING OF THINGS IN DIFFERENT WAYS

Read Aloud Activity

For the teacher: The purpose of flexible thinking is to generate ideas which deviate from the obvious patterns. This is a shift in how we look at things and how we use items currently. Examples of questions which encourage flexible thinking are the following:

- ❏ What else could we use this for?
- ❏ What is another way of looking at this?
- ❏ Analogies: _____ is to _____ as _____ is to _____.
- ❏ What relationship can you think of between _____ and _____?

- ❏ Begin to read aloud *The Turn About, Think About, Look About Book* by Beau Gardner.
- ❏ As you read each page, ask students what they think each picture represents. Then reveal what the author/illustrator labeled the picture.
- ❏ As you read, ask leading questions such as: What new labels could you give these pictures?
- ❏ Be sure to stress that as the book is turned, the viewpoint changes and so does the picture.
- ❏ Distribute the Read Aloud Reflection page (Handout 2.2).
- ❏ Direct students to carefully consider and answer the questions on the top half. When students have finished, discuss as a whole group. Students may add additional information to their answers after the discussion. Key understandings for the read aloud are outlined in Box 2.1.
- ❏ Tell students now it's their turn to think flexibly. Look at the shape below. Draw a scene using this shape as a part of your picture. Then create an abstract title.

Box 2.1: *The Turn About, Think About, Look About Book* Key Understandings

- ❏ This book shows how changing the visual perspective can completely change the image portrayed. This allows the reader to look at things from a variety of viewpoints and angles, and to shift one's train of thought to produce a variety of ideas. Both *Round Trip* and *The Turn About, Think About, Look About Book* show how changing the visual perspective can change the image portrayed.
- ❏ The author showed flexible thinking by creating illustrations that can be viewed from various perspectives and in turn be seen as completely different objects.

Handout 2.2: Read Aloud Reflection
The Turn About, Think About, Look About Book by Beau Gardner

Name: _____

In what ways are *Round Trip* and the *Turn About, Think About, Look About Book* the same?	How did the author show flexible thinking?

Now it's your turn to think flexibly. Look at the shape below. Draw a scene using this shape as a part of your picture. Then create an abstract title.

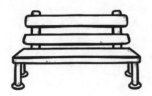

Skill Development Activity

❑ Tell students they are going to add pages to *The Turn About, Think About, Look About Book*.

❑ Divide students into groups of four. Distribute the Varying Viewpoints pages (Handout 2.3.a–d) so that each person in the group has a different page.

❑ Read the directions to the students and model how to rotate the paper to see the illustration from different perspectives. Look at the item in the center of the box. Next to the number 1, write what you think it looks like. Then turn your page so that the number 2 is facing you, and write down a new idea. Continue turning your paper and generating new ideas based on your new perspective.

❑ Once everyone has recorded their four new ideas, tell the students with the same image to gather in a circle.

❑ Students will take turns sharing their perspectives and explaining what they saw when they rotated the paper.

❑ Bring everyone back together to discuss how various people saw different things using the same stimulus. Ask students how this activity used flexible thinking.

Changing Perspectives Lesson 2: Understanding Others' Points of View

Objective: Apply flexibility of thought when understanding the viewpoints of others.

Materials

❑ *The Day the Crayons Quit* by Drew Daywalt (teacher's copy)
❑ Handout 2.4: Read Aloud Reflection (one per student)
❑ Handout 2.5: Viewing Photographs from Various Perspectives (one per student)
❑ Photographs from Unsplash (enlarged either with a document camera or by copying and printing in large format)
   ■ Highbridge in the mountains https://unsplash.com/photos/44m2xJxQvkE
   ■ Bees: https://unsplash.com/photos/6ufBhNungOk

Handout 2.3.a: Varying Viewpoints

Name: _____

DIRECTIONS: Look at the item in the center of the box. Next to the number one write what you think it looks like. Then turn you page so that the number 2 is facing you, write down a new idea. Continue turning your paper and generating new ideas based on your new perspective.

Handout 2.3.b: Varying Viewpoints

Name: _____

DIRECTIONS: Look at the item in the center of the box. Next to the number one write what you think it looks like. Then turn you page so that the number 2 is facing you, write down a new idea. Continue turning your paper and generating new ideas based on your new perspective.

Handout 2.3.c: Varying Viewpoints

Name: _____

DIRECTIONS: Look at the item in the center of the box. Next to the number one write what you think it looks like. Then turn you page so that the number 2 is facing you, write down a new idea. Continue turning your paper and generating new ideas based on your new perspective.

3

2

4

1

1

Handout 2.3.d: Varying Viewpoints

Name: _____

DIRECTIONS: Look at the item in the center of the box. Next to the number one write what you think it looks like. Then turn you page so that the number 2 is facing you, write down a new idea. Continue turning your paper and generating new ideas based on your new perspective.

3

2

4

1

- ■ Tiered farmland: https://unsplash.com/photos/6Z_S-2UWzmA
- ■ People at a concert: https://unsplash.com/photos/y4MgW_OGQ28
- ❏ Handout 2.6: Socratic Seminar Graphic Organizer (one per student)

Whole Group Introduction

- ❏ Ask students, "What would you rather be? And why?"
  - ■ A bike or a skateboard?
  - ■ A baby or a grandparent?
  - ■ A square or a circle?
- ❏ Review the creative thinking skill Changing Perspectives Anchor Chart. Tell students they were just using flexible thinking when they played "What would you rather be?" Remind students that changing perspective is the ability to flexibly look at things from a variety of perspectives and angles, or to shift one's train of thought to produce a variety of ideas. Often flexible thinking occurs when forcing two seemingly different ideas together or when constraints prevent production of a simple solution.
- ❏ Tell the students that today they will be thinking flexibly about various people's perspectives.

Read Aloud Activity

- ❏ Ask students, "What makes someone quit a job? A sport? Reading a certain book?" Tell students that in the story you are about to read, each character has a different reason for quitting.
- ❏ Read aloud the story *The Day the Crayons Quit* by Drew Daywalt. The crayons each explain why they have had enough and are quitting.
- ❏ As you read, pause to ask students about perspective. You may choose to use questions such as: Why does _____ want to quit? Why does _____ claim they are the color of the sun? Who is correct? How can a different point of view reveal personality traits?
- ❏ Distribute the Read Aloud Reflection page (Handout 2.4). Allow students to work in partners or alone to answer the questions. Key understandings for the read aloud are outlined in Box 2.2.

Handout 2.4: Read Aloud Reflection
The Day the Crayons Quit by Drew Daywalt

Name: _____

Give a brief summary of the events of the book. You can make a list, timeline, or write a few sentences.

- -

What caused the crayons to quit?

Which crayon do you believe has the strongest argument for quitting? Explain.

Pick a crayon. How does their point of view reveal personality traits?

Box 2.2: *The Day the Crayons Quit* Key Understandings

❏ *Give a summary of the events of the book.*
  ■ Duncan receives letters from each of his crayons explaining why they are unsatisfied with how they are being used. Each crayon provides reasons as to why they're upset and states they are going on strike. Duncan finds a creative way to use each crayon in a new and unique way.

❏ *What caused the crayons to quit?*
  ■ They were all dissatisfied with how and what they were being used for.

❏ *Which crayon do you believe has the strongest argument for quitting? Explain.*
  ■ Accept all reasonable answers.

❏ *Pick a crayon; how does their point of view reflect their personality?*
  ■ The purple crayon is upset that Duncan uses him outside of the lines; this could reflect perfectionism. (Accept any answer that can be explained.)

Skill Development Activity

❏ Distribute Viewing Photographs from Various Perspectives (Handout 2.5). Tell students they will be viewing photographs through various "people's" eyes. As students observe each photograph, they will analyze the image from four various viewpoints asking the question: How might the following people react to this image?

❏ At the time of publication, these images were available on the website Unsplash. If they are no longer available, you may simply find pictures of a high bridge, bees, farmland, and people at a concert.

❏ Project the photograph of the bridge in the high mountains. Ask students to share what they observe in this photograph.

❏ Now we will look at this picture by imagining how various people would view this same picture.
  ■ How would an engineer, or one who designs and builds complex structures, view this bridge?
  ■ How might a seismologist, or a scientist who studies earthquakes, view this bridge?

Handout 2.5: Viewing Photographs from Various Perspectives

Name: _____

BRIDGE	Engineer (designs structures)	Seismologist (studies earthquakes)	Trucker	Helicopter tours
BEES	Beekeeper (farms bees)	Someone who's allergic to bees	A flower	A grocer
FARM	Real Estate Developer (wants land)	Farmer (money from crops)	Hiker	Environmentalist (protects the environment)
CONCERT	Artist (singer)	Infectious Disease Scientist (studies germs)	Someone who is claustrophobic (scared of confined spaces)	Venue owner (place of concert)

- How might a trucker, the driver of an 18-wheeler, view this bridge?
- How might a guide on helicopters tours view this picture?
❏ Continue in the same manner for the rest of the photographs. Model asking the questions based on the various perspectives and clarifying the role of each perspective.
❏ Discuss how the various pictures were seen differently depending upon who was looking at the photograph. The person's role, personality, perspective, knowledge, and understanding may elicit different responses to the same image.

Concluding Socratic Seminar

❏ After the Viewing Photographs from Various Perspectives activity, conduct a Socratic seminar on the following focus question: "How does this lesson relate to the real world? Is it always beneficial to look at things from others' perspectives?"

TABLE 2.2
Possible Answers for Viewing Photographs from Various Perspectives

bridge	An engineer would look to see if the bridge was structurally strong.	A seismologist would look to see if there was a fault line anywhere close.	A truck driver may be nervous about driving on the high bridge.	A person who gives helicopter tours may love the view.
bees	A beekeeper would love to see healthy bees.	A person allergic to bees may want to make sure they have an epi-pen near.	A flower would be happy to see the bees; they will continue to be pollinated.	A grocer would want to see a strong bee colony that can make honey for their store.
farm	A real estate developer may want to buy the land to build a neighborhood.	A farmer would want to keep growing crops on the land.	A hiker may want to hike through the farmland because it has unique terrain.	An environmentalist would want to keep the land free from chemicals.
concert	The artist playing would be happy to perform and make money.	An infectious-disease scientist may not want the people so close together.	Someone who is claustrophobic may not like all the people crowded around.	A concert venue owner would like all the money the concert will generate.

What Is a Socratic Seminar?

❑ Socratic seminar is a teaching strategy that provides students the opportunity to discuss a topic or concept to gain a deeper understanding. Socrates believed that students learn best when provided the opportunity to come to an understanding themselves through thoughtful questioning. Socrates did not provide answers to his students' questions; rather, he responded to questions with more questions. This allowed the students to examine their own thinking and come to their own conclusions.

The Socratic Method

❑ Requires all students to feel safe to contribute to the discussion; team-building must occur before attempting a seminar.

❑ Uses questions to examine values and beliefs focusing on moral education as well as information.

❑ Demands a classroom environment characterized by "productive discomfort."

❑ Is used to demonstrate complexity and uncertainty in our world.

Teacher's Role

❑ The teacher is the facilitator. The role of the teacher in a Socratic Seminar shifts from the "Sage on the Stage" to the "Guide on the Side." As the teacher, you must guide the students through further questioning and create a shared dialogue.

❑ Find a space where all students can face each other, either moving their desks into a circle or sitting on the floor in a circle.

❑ Set dialogue guidelines. Participation requires students to be active listeners. Ask students to connect their statements with those before them using phrases like "I agree with…because…" or "I respectfully disagree with…because…" Remind students that they are encouraged to ask one another questions.

❑ Teach students about natural lulls in conversation and when it is appropriate to begin their next statement. Also talk about conversation "hogs" and "logs." A "hog" talks the entire time and doesn't allow others to speak. A "log" is someone who doesn't speak and allows the conversation to take place without their voice. In a Socratic Seminar, all people should have the opportunity to share their thoughts.

❑ Allow for wait time. Silence is not the enemy! Let students sit with a question for at least 10 seconds without rephrasing it. Students need time to grapple with challenging questions.

❏ Encourage students to take ownership of the conversation. Students should ask one another questions to clarify and feel comfortable asking the group a new question to further the discussion.

❏ The teacher may interject with either quick teaching moments, clarifying statements, or additional questions; however, this approach should be used with caution so as not to take over the dialogue.

Box 2.3: Socratic Seminar Prompting Questions

❏ Who can offer a different perspective?
❏ Can you please support that statement with evidence from the text?
❏ Can you clarify your statement?
❏ Who hasn't had a chance to speak yet?
❏ Has anyone had a change of heart?
❏ Who has changed their point of view?
❏ What piece of evidence made you change your opinion?
❏ Can anyone give a counter-argument?
❏ How can you relate this to your own life?
❏ Who else should read this piece? Why?
❏ Why is this information important?
❏ Do you agree or disagree with the author?
❏ What other evidence would you need to change your mind?
❏ What else can you tell us about … ?
❏ What makes you say/think … ?

Implementation

❏ Go over Socratic Seminar guidelines and expectations.

Box 2.4: Socratic Seminar Guidelines

1. *All participants must come prepared.*
   ■ Read the text(s) carefully.
   ■ Take notes.
   ■ Complete the Preparation Page.

2. *Be an active participant and listener.*
   - Listen to what others say and don't interrupt.
   - Try to connect your idea to others.
   - "I agree with...because..."
   - "I respectfully disagree with...because..."
   - Ask clarifying questions when needed.

3. *Speak clearly.*
   - State your opinion or idea in concise language.
   - Provide text evidence when possible.

4. *Be respectful.*
   - Speak only when it is your turn.
   - You don't have to raise your hand, but wait for your turn to talk.
   - This is an exchange of ideas, not a debate.

❑ Allow students time to prepare. Distribute the Socratic Seminar Graphic Organizer (Handout 2.6) and allow students time to jot down their notes/ideas in the "I think...because..." section. Tell students they will have 10–15 minutes to gather their thoughts on the focus questions: How does this lesson relate to the real world? Is it always beneficial to look at things through others' perspectives?

❑ Before facilitating the Socratic Seminar, go over possible sentence starters.

Box 2.5: Socratic Seminar Sentence Starters

❑ I agree with...because...
❑ I respectfully disagree with...because...
❑ I wonder...
❑ Based on page...I think...
❑ I also noticed...
❑ I can infer...
❑ On page...it says...
❑ I understand what you are saying, but...
❑ Can you clarify that last statement?
❑ I don't understand...
❑ I am curious...
❑ What makes you say...?

Handout 2.6: Socratic Seminar Graphic Organizer

Name: _____

Socratic Seminar Question

Now we will discuss some focus questions to help us better understand:

How does this lesson relate to the real world?

I THINK...

BECAUSE

BECAUSE

BECAUSE

After the discussion, my answer (changed/stayed the same) because...

_____
_____
_____
_____

❑ Facilitate the Socratic Seminar. The teacher poses the focus question: How does this lesson relate to the real world? Allow students to share their insights. As the conversation comes to a natural lull, guide students to a deeper understanding by asking the follow-up questions: How/When is it beneficial to look at something through another's eyes? Can you give an example of a time you needed to view something from someone else's perspective? Remember that wait time is key, remind students to respect various viewpoints, and allow time for cognitive dissonance.

❑ After the seminar, provide a debrief of what you heard throughout the conversation. Summarize the main points to ensure learning. Finally, have students complete the final section on the Socratic Seminar Graphic Organizer.

❑ **Student Grouping:** Groups should be based on the goals for student learning as well as student readiness levels. Two suggested groupings are the following:

■ Whole class—Invite the whole class to sit in a circle and participate in the discussion.

■ Inside/outside circle—In this version, half of the class sits on the inside and participates in the seminar. The rest of the students sit on the outside of the circle and take notes on what is being discussed. Then the students switch roles. This is a great way to differentiate through using one of the following grouping strategies:

1. Strategically plan to have the quieter students together during the first inside circle, which will force them to participate.
2. Have the highly verbal students participate first, allowing more hesitant students a chance to hear the dialogue before requiring them to participate.

❑ **Assessment:** Overall performance and deep thinking based on discussion participation and student thinking framework responses should be informally assessed throughout the unit. Rubrics are available in Appendix A.

■ **Socratic Seminar Rubric:** Quickly assess student participation and preparedness along a continuum to show growth.

■ **Socratic Seminar Self-Reflection:** Students evaluate their own participation and levels of thinking through the seminar process.

Changing Perspectives Authentic Application Activity: Circle of Viewpoints

Objective: Apply flexibility of thought when changing viewpoints.

Materials

- ❏ Handout 2.7: Jack and the Beanstalk (one per student)
- ❏ Handout 2.8: Read Aloud Reflection (one per student)
- ❏ Handout 2.9: Circle of Viewpoints (one per student)

Whole Group Introduction

- ❏ Ask students: Can someone be both a hero and a villain? Explain. If students are having trouble generating ideas, prompt the students with the idea of Robin Hood stealing from the rich to give to the poor, or Maleficent, who was a good fairy but turned evil after circumstances in her life. Allow for time to discuss if the characters' heroic acts outweigh their villainous acts.
- ❏ Review the creative thinking skill Changing Perspectives Anchor Chart. Tell students they were just using flexible thinking when they discussed the idea of a character being both "good" and "bad." Remind students that changing perspectives is the ability to flexibly look at things from a variety of perspectives and angles, or to shift one's train of thought to produce a variety of ideas. Often flexible thinking occurs when forcing two seemingly different ideas together or when constraints prevent production of a simple solution.

Tell the students that today they will be reading about a character with both heroic and villainous characteristics.

Read Aloud Activity

- ❏ Hand out student copies of *Jack and the Beanstalk* (Handout 2.7). Ask students to read along with you. After the initial read, ask students: Who is the good guy and who is the bad guy in this story? Allow students to determine that there is no clear good guy/bad guy.
- ❏ Distribute the Read Aloud Reflection Page (Handout 2.8). Direct students to carefully consider and answer the questions. When students have finished, discuss responses as a whole group. Key understandings for this read aloud are outlined in Box 2.6.

Handout 2.7: *Jack and the Beanstalk*

Name: _____

There was once upon a time a poor widow who had an only son named Jack, and a cow named Milky-white. And all they had to live on was the milk the cow gave every morning, which they carried to the market and sold. But one morning Milky-white gave no milk and they didn't know what to do.

"What shall we do, what shall we do?" said the widow, wringing her hands.

"Cheer up, mother, I'll go and get work somewhere," said Jack.

"We've tried that before, and nobody would take you," said his mother; "we must sell Milky-white and with the money do something, start shop, or something."

"All right, mother," says Jack; "it's market-day today, and I'll soon sell Milky-white, and then we'll see what we can do."

So, he took the cow's halter in his hand, and off he started. He hadn't gone far when he met a funny-looking old man who said to him: "Good morning, Jack."

"Good morning to you," said Jack, and wondered how he knew his name.

"Well, Jack, and where are you off to?" said the man.

"I'm going to market to sell our cow here."

"Oh, you look the proper sort of chap to sell cows," said the man; "I wonder if you know how many beans make five."

"Two in each hand and one in your mouth," says Jack, as sharp as a needle.

"Right you are," said the man, "and here they are the very beans themselves," he went on pulling out of his pocket a number of strange- looking beans. "As you are so sharp," says he, "I don't mind doing a swop with you–your cow for these beans."

"Walker!" says Jack, "wouldn't you like it?"

"Ah! you don't know what these beans are," said the man, "if you plant them over-night, by morning they grow right up to the sky."

"Really?" says Jack, "you don't say so."

"Yes, that is so, and if it doesn't turn out to be true you can have your cow back."

"Right," says Jack, and hands him over Milky-white's halter and pockets the beans.

Back goes Jack home, and as he hadn't gone very far it wasn't dusk by the time, he got to his door.

"What back, Jack?" said his mother, "I see you haven't got Milky- white, so you've sold her. How much did you get for her?"

"You'll never guess, mother," says Jack.

"No, you don't say so. Good boy! Five pounds, ten, fifteen, no, it can't be twenty."

"I told you, you couldn't guess, what do you say to these beans; they're magical, plant them over-night and—"

"What!" says Jack's mother, "have you been such a fool, such a dolt, such an idiot, as to give away my Milky-white, the best milker in the parish, and prime beef to boot, for a set of paltry beans. Take that! Take that! Take that! And as for your precious beans here they go out of the window. And now off with you to bed. Not a sip shall you drink, and not a bit shall you swallow this very night."

So, Jack went upstairs to his little room in the attic, and sad and sorry he was, to be sure, as much for his mother's sake, as for the loss of his supper.

At last, he dropped off to sleep.

When he woke up, the room looked so funny. The sun was shining into part of it, and yet all the rest was quite dark and shady. So, Jack jumped up and dressed himself and went to the window. And what do you think he saw? Why, the beans his mother had thrown out of the window into the garden had sprung up into a big beanstalk, which went up and up and up till it reached the sky. So, the man spoke truth after all.

The beanstalk grew up quite close past Jack's window, so all he had to do was to open it and give a jump on to the beanstalk, which was made like a big plaited ladder. So, Jack climbed, and he climbed, and he climbed, and he climbed, and he climbed, and he climbed, and he climbed till at last he reached the sky. And when he got there, he found a long broad road going as straight as a dart. So, he walked along, and he walked along, and he walked along till he came to a great big tall house, and on the doorstep, there was a great big tall woman.

"Good morning, mum," says Jack, quite polite-like. "Could you be so kind as to give me some breakfast?" For he had not had anything to eat, you know, the night before and was as hungry as a hunter.

"It's breakfast you want, is it?" says the great big tall woman, "it's breakfast you'll be if you don't move off from here. My man is an ogre and there is nothing he likes better than boys broiled on toast. You'd better be moving on or he'll soon be coming."

"Oh! Please mum, do give me something to eat, mum. I've had nothing to eat since yesterday morning, really and truly, mum," says Jack. "I may as well be broiled, as die of hunger."

Well, the ogre's wife was not such a bad sort, after all. So, she took Jack into the kitchen and gave him a chunk of bread and cheese and a jug of milk. But Jack hadn't half-finished these when thump! Thump! Thump! The whole house began to tremble with the noise of someone coming.

Handout 2.7, continued: *Jack and the Beanstalk*

"I, Goodness gracious me! It's my old man," said the ogre's wife, "what on earth shall I do? Here, come quick and jump in here." And she bundled Jack into the oven just as the ogre came in.

He was a big one, to be sure. At his belt, he had three calves strung up by the heels, and he unhooked them, threw them down on the table, and said, "Here, wife, broil me a couple of these for breakfast. Ah, what's this I smell?

"Fee-fi-fo-fum,

I smell the blood of an Englishman,

Be he alive, or be he dead

I'll have his bones to grind my bread."

"Nonsense, dear," said his wife, "you're dreaming. Or perhaps you smell the scraps of that little boy you liked so much for yesterday's dinner. Here, go you and have a wash and tidy up, and by the time you come back your breakfast'll be ready for you."

So, the ogre went off, and Jack was just going to jump out of the oven and run off when the woman told him not. "Wait till he's asleep," says she, "he always has a snooze after breakfast."

Well, the ogre had his breakfast, and after that he goes to a big chest and takes out of it a couple of bags of gold and sits down counting them till at last his head began to nod and he began to snore till the whole house shook again.

Then Jack crept out on tiptoe from his oven, and as he was passing the ogre, he took one of the bags of gold under his arm, and off he ran till he came to the beanstalk. Then he threw down the bag of gold which of course fell into his mother's garden, and then he climbed down and climbed down till at last he got home and told his mother and showed her the gold and said, "Well, mother, wasn't I right about the beans. They are really magical, you see."

So, they lived on the bag of gold for some time, but at last, they came to the end of that, so Jack made up his mind to try his luck once more up at the top of the beanstalk. So, one fine morning he got up early, and got on to the beanstalk, and he climbed, and he climbed, and he climbed, and he climbed, and he climbed, and he climbed till at last he got on the road again and came to the great big tall house he had been to before. There, sure enough, was the great big tall woman a-standing on the doorstep.

"Good morning, mum," says Jack, as bold as brass, "could you be so good as to give me something to eat?"

"Go away, my boy," said the big, tall woman, "or else my man will eat you up for breakfast. But aren't you the youngster who came here once before? Do you know that very day; my man missed one of his bags of gold."

3

Handout 2.7, continued: *Jack and the Beanstalk*

"That's strange, mum," says Jack, "I dare say I could tell you something about that but I'm so hungry I can't speak till I've had something to eat."

Well, the big tall woman was that curious that she took him in and gave him something to eat. But he had scarcely begun munching it as slowly as he could when thump! Thump! Thump! They heard the giant's footstep, and his wife hid Jack away in the oven.

All happened as it did before. In came the ogre as he did before, said: "Fee-fi-fo-fum," and had his breakfast off three broiled oxen. Then he said, "Wife, bring me the hen that lays the golden eggs." So, she brought it, and the ogre said, "Lay," and it laid an egg all of gold. Then the ogre began to nod his head, and to snore till the house shook.

Then Jack crept out of the oven on tiptoe and caught hold of the golden hen and was off before you could say "Jack Robinson." But this time the hen gave a cackle, which woke the ogre, and just as Jack got out of the house, he heard him calling: "Wife, wife, what have you done with my golden hen?"

And the wife said, "Why, my dear?"

But that was all Jack heard, for he rushed off to the beanstalk and climbed down like a house on fire. And when he got home, he showed his mother the wonderful hen and said "Lay," to it; and it laid a golden egg every time he said, "Lay."

Well, Jack was not content, and it wasn't very long before he determined to have another try at his luck up there at the top of the beanstalk. So, one fine morning, he got up early, and went on to the beanstalk, and he climbed, and he climbed, and he climbed, and he climbed till he got to the top. But this time he knew better than to go straight to the ogre's house. And when he got near it, he waited behind a bush till he saw the ogre's wife come out with a pail to get some water, and then he crept into the house and got into the copper. He hadn't been there long when he heard Thump! Thump! Thump! As before, and in come the ogre and his wife.

"Fee-fi-fo-fum, I smell the blood of an Englishman," cried out the ogre; "I smell him, wife, I smell him."

"Do you, my dearie?" says the ogre's wife. "Then if it's that little rogue that stole your gold and the hen that laid the golden eggs, he's sure to have got into the oven." And they both rushed to the oven. But Jack wasn't there, luckily, and the ogre's wife said, "There you are again with your fee-fi-fo-fum. Why of course it's the laddie you caught last night that I've broiled for your breakfast. How forgetful I am, and how careless you are not to tell the difference between a live one and a dead one."

So, the ogre sat down to the breakfast and ate it, but every now and then, he would mutter: "Well, I could have sworn—" and he'd get up and search the larder and the cupboards, and everything, only luckily, he didn't think of the copper.

After breakfast was over, the ogre called out, "Wife, wife, bring me my golden harp." So, she brought it and put it on the table before him. Then he said, "Sing!" and the golden harp sang most beautifully. And it went on singing till the ogre fell asleep and commenced to snore like thunder.

Then Jack lifted the copper-lid very quietly, got down like a mouse, and crept on hands and knees till he got to the table when he got up and caught hold of the golden harp and dashed with it towards the door. But the harp called out quite loud: "Master! Master!" and the ogre woke up just in time to see Jack running off with his harp.

Jack ran as fast as he could, and the ogre came rushing after, and would soon have caught him only Jack had a start and dodged him a bit and knew where he was going. When he got to the beanstalk the ogre was not more than twenty yards away when suddenly he saw Jack disappear, and when he got up to the end of the road, he saw Jack underneath climbing down for dear life. Well, the ogre didn't like trusting himself to such a ladder, and he stood and waited, so Jack got another start. But just then, the harp cried out, "Master! Master!" and the ogre swung himself down on to the beanstalk, which shook with his weight. Down climbed Jack, and after him climbed the ogre. By this time, Jack had climbed down, and climbed down, and climbed down till he was very nearly home. So, he called out, "Mother! Mother! Bring me an axe, bring me an axe." And his mother came rushing out with the axe in her hand, but when she came to the beanstalk, she stood stock still with fright for there she saw the ogre just coming down below the clouds.

But Jack jumped down, got hold of the axe, and gave a chop at the beanstalk, which cut it half in two. The ogre felt the beanstalk shake and quiver, so he stopped to see what the matter was. Then Jack gave another chop with the axe, and the beanstalk was cut in two and began to topple over. Then the ogre fell down and broke his crown, and the beanstalk came toppling after.

Then Jack showed his mother his golden harp, and what with showing that and selling the golden eggs, Jack and his mother became very rich, and he married a great princess, and they lived happy ever after.

Handout 2.8: Read Aloud Reflection

Jack and the Beanstalk

Name: _____

What rules does Jack break?

What rules does the giant break?

Whose actions are worse? Explain.

Pick a character who shows a pattern of behavior. Describe the pattern. Does this pattern get better or worse over time?

Talk about the perspective of the giant, the giant's wife, and Jack. How are these different?

Box 2.6: *Jack and the Beanstalk* Key Understandings

❑ Initially after reading the story, many people think Jack is a hero. He has rid the world of a man-eating giant. However, if you look at Jack's actions, he breaks many societal rules. Jack steals, lies, is greedy, and kills the giant.

❑ Some may even claim the giant is a victim of Jack's actions. The giant is the victim of multiple thefts, and in the end he dies.

❑ Some may say that Jack's actions are worse because he steals multiple times due to his greed, he lies, and he kills, whereas the giant only ate people. Others may say a human's life is worth far more than a giant's, and breaking rules to rid the world of the giant is excusable.

❑ Jack's pattern of lying and stealing increases. At first, he only steals a bag of gold, and then he becomes greedier and continues to steal more and more.

❑ The giant's pattern of hunting and eating children seems to stay the same throughout.

❑ Each character is mainly concerned with their own well-being; they don't look at the issue from the other's perspective.

Application Activity

❑ Distribute the Circle of Viewpoints (Handout 2.9). Tell students they will be looking at the question: Should Jack be prosecuted for stealing the golden goose? Explain that to complete the circle of viewpoints, they will have to put themselves in both Jack's and the Giant's shoes.

❑ You may wish to project this graphic organizer and model how to complete the perspectives of Jack and the Giant. Tell the students that first, they will take on the perspective of Jack. Record reasons for or against prosecution. Make sure to provide any evidence from the text to support Jack's perspective. Record events from the text and reasons in the corresponding section of the Circle of Viewpoints.

■ Jack needed money and food for his family.

■ He only stole a few times, and the person he stole from was a bad giant.

■ He was only ridding the world of a man-eating giant.

Handout 2.9: Circle of Viewpoints

Name: _____

Answer the question below by putting yourself into the shoes of the characters.

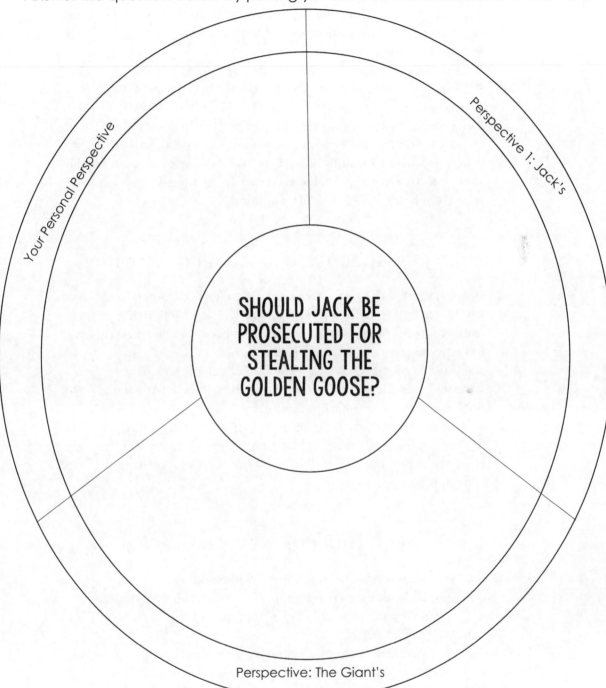

Your Personal Perspective

Perspective 1: Jack's

SHOULD JACK BE PROSECUTED FOR STEALING THE GOLDEN GOOSE?

Perspective: The Giant's

❑ Tell the students that now they will put themselves in the mindset of the Giant. Record text evidence and reasons for or against prosecution from the giant's perspective. Record events from the text and reasons in the corresponding section of the Circle of Viewpoints.
   ■ There is no excuse for stealing.
   ■ The giant lost many precious items due to Jack's theft.
   ■ Clearly the golden goose loved the giant because he called out to his master.
❑ Now students will record their own perspective. Remind students that they must provide text evidence to support their perspective.
❑ Follow up with a turn-and-talk or brief whole group discussion for closure. Ask students: How did your viewpoint change when you placed yourself in Jack's shoes? The Giant's shoes?

Changing Perspectives Concluding Activities

❑ Distribute the Changing Perspectives Exit Ticket (Appendix A). Ask students to reflect on their learning about the skill of changing perspectives. Allow time for students to complete the exit ticket. Use this as a formative assessment to gain a better understanding of your students' readiness to effectively practice the skill of perspective.
❑ If desired, complete the Group Observation Rubric (Appendix A) to track students' progress with the skill.
❑ Ask students to retrieve their Divergent Thinking Avatar (Handout I.5). In the Changing Perspectives box, they should either record the main ideas about the thinking skill or illustrate their avatar using the skill of perspective.

Bibliography

Bees Photo by: https://unsplash.com/photos/6ufBhNungOk.

Daywalt, D. (2014). *The day the crayons quit*. New York: Philomel Books.

Gardner, B. (1980). *The turn about, think about, look about book*. New York: William Morrow & Co.

High bridge photo by: https://unsplash.com/photos/44m2xJxQvkE.

People at a concert by: https://unsplash.com/photos/y4MgW_OGQ28.

Tiered farmland photo by: https://unsplash.com/photos/6Z_S-2UWzmA.

CHAPTER 3

Sub-Skill 3

Elaborating

TABLE 3.1
Elaborating Sub-Skill Overview

Thinking Skill Outline	
Focus Questions	❏ What else could you (add/tell/improve) about this idea? ❏ Can you be more descriptive?
Lesson 1	*Visual Elaboration* ❏ **Trade Book Focus:** *The Dot* by Peter H. Reynolds ❏ **Practice Activity:** Students will use various art mediums to elaborate a dot picture.
Lesson 2	*Elaborating in Writing* ❏ **Trade Book Focus:** *Little Red Writing* by Joan Holub ❏ **Practice Activity:** Creating a shared writing piece focused on adding details.
Authentic Application Activity	*Using Elaboration in Opinion Writing* ❏ **Practice Activity:** Students write to the prompt: Should there be homework?

DOI: 10.4324/9781003267959-4

Elaborating Lesson 1: Visual Elaboration

Objective: Discover how adding details to art can make it more interesting.

Materials

- ❏ Handout 3.1: Elaboration Anchor Chart (one enlarged copy for the class)
- ❏ Handout 3.2: What is Elaborating? (one per student)
- ❏ *The Dot* by Peter H. Reynolds (teacher's copy)
- ❏ Handout 3.3 Read Aloud Reflection page (one per student)
- ❏ Construction paper
- ❏ Black dot stickers (or you can simply draw a black dot on the construction paper)
- ❏ Art materials

Whole Group Introduction

- ❏ Tell students the story, "Once there was a poor boy who killed a giant and got rich. The End." Ask students what was wrong with that story. It lacks details and is boring.
- ❏ Tell the students that they are going to create a new and descriptive story. Each person will have a chance to add a sentence to our story. Begin the story circle with the sentence, "Oh no, what was that noise?" Have students go around the circle adding new ideas and details to the story.
- ❏ Introduce the creative thinking skill using the Elaboration Anchor Chart (Handout 3.1). Tell students they just created a story using elaborative thinking. Elaboration is the creative thinking process of adding details or expanding on ideas. It is the ability to build up and embellish ideas to make the idea more interesting. Examples of questions which encourage elaboration are the following:
  - ■ What else can you (add/tell me/improve) about this idea?
  - ■ Can you be more descriptive?
- ❏ A vocabulary lesson is provided for students to learn the different forms of the word *elaborate*. In this unit, the various forms of the word will be used, and this lesson will build schema before students are expected to apply the word.

ELABORATING

ADDING DETAILS TO IDEAS TO BUILD THEM UP

❏ Distribute What is Elaborating? (Handout 3.2). Explain that the word *elaborate* has various word forms and, depending on the suffix, it can be a noun, verb, adjective, or adverb. Remind students:
  ■ A noun is a person, place, thing, or idea.
  ■ A verb is an action.
  ■ An adjective describes the noun.
  ■ An adverb describes how or what the verb is doing.

❏ Read the definitions and sentence with the students. Discuss the sentence and decide which form of the word fits. Discuss how the word becomes a different form depending on how it is used in a sentence.

❏ Tell students to cut out the words at the bottom, determine which form of the word fits each definition and sentence, then place the word under the sentence. Circulate and check for understanding before allowing students to glue down their answers.

Read Aloud Activity

❏ Tell students you will be reading a book in which the character also uses elaborative thinking. Read the book *The Dot* by Peter H. Reynolds. This book follows the story of a little girl as she discovers her creativity by adding ideas to her very first piece of artwork, a simple dot. After reading, ask students, "How does this book show elaborative thinking?"

❏ Distribute the Read Aloud Reflection Page (Handout 3.3). Direct students to carefully consider and answer the questions. When students have finished, discuss responses as a whole group. Allow students time to share their picture scenes, emphasizing that the greater detail added to the scene makes the picture tell a more complete story.

Box 3.1: *The Dot* Key Understandings

❏ Vashti is stuck; she believes she is not an artist. Her teacher gently encourages her to make a mark and see where it takes her. Vashti becomes angry and jabs a dot on her paper. Much to her surprise, the teacher tells her to sign the piece. The teacher frames her dot and with that little bit of encouragement, Vashti decides to elaborate and do better. She explores with paint, elaborating different colors, sizes, and shapes. Vashti learns that she is an artist and goes on to encourage others.

Handout 3.2: What is ELABORATING?

Name: _____

To add details to; expand ideas

Picasso _____ his collage by adding more details.

verb

Worked out with a great care to detail

The Mona Lisa is an _____ painting.

Adj.

The state of being elaborated

The novel was an _____ of a short story.

noun

The act of elaborating

Georges Braque _____ painted *The Portuguese*.

adverb

elaborated   elaborate   elaboration   elaborately

Handout 3.3: Read Aloud Reflection
The Dot by Peter H. Reynolds

Name: _____

Summarize the main idea of "The Dot".	How did the character show elaboration?

Create a scene below using the video camera as a main part. Answer the questions: Who is doing the taping? What are they taping? Why are they videotaping? Where are they?

Skill Development Activity

❑ Remind students that creative thinkers are *imaginative*, *original*, and *flexible* in their thinking, allowing their ideas to blossom and form freely. Creative thinkers also collaborate with others. This sharing of ideas allows for *fluency*, or a greater number of ideas. As the ideas form, the creative mind looks for combinations and *elaborates* on the idea, adding details to create something new and unique. Explain that artists often use elaboration when they are trying to convey meaning of emotion in a piece. Artists will choose specific colors, shapes, lines, movement, and textures to express their ideas.

❑ Give each student a blank piece of construction or art paper. Tell them to put a dot (either a dot sticker or just with a black crayon or marker) somewhere on the paper and sign it.

❑ Next, get out a variety of art mediums (crayons, markers, pastels, watercolor, glitter, sequins, etc.) Tell the students to add detail to their masterpiece.

❑ When they have completed their picture, give them an index card on which to title and describe their piece. Encourage students to describe their process, mediums, color choices and the feelings the piece may evoke.

Elaborating Lesson 2: Elaborating in Writing

Objective: Learn how adding descriptive words enhances a piece of writing.

Materials

❑ Image of a bird link: https://unsplash.com/photos/RLLROoRz16Y.
❑ *Little Red Writing* by Joan Holub (teacher's copy)
❑ Handout 3.4: Read Aloud Reflection (one per student)
❑ Lollipop for each student
❑ Poster paper or a document camera to record the shared writing piece
❑ Handout 3.5: Elaboration Pre-Writing Chart (teacher's copy)
❑ Optional Handout 3.6: Elaboration Paragraph Frame

Whole Group Introduction

❑ Remind students that elaborative thinking requires adding details or expanding on an idea. It is the ability to build up and embellish ideas to make the idea more interesting.

❑ Elaboration in writing is the process of further developing an idea. It requires adding additional details to better explain what has already been said. Examples of questions which encourage elaboration are the following:
  - What else can you (add/tell me/improve) about this idea?
  - Can you be more descriptive?

❑ Display a photograph of a bird or use the link listed in the materials to access a sample picture.

❑ Then write the sentence, *This is a bird.* Ask students:
  - Is this a sentence? Yes, it has a subject and a verb.
  - Is it interesting? No, it's boring.
  - Would someone who is not looking at this picture be able to describe the bird? No.

❑ Have students help you write a better, more descriptive sentence. Use the following question stems:
  - What adjectives describe the bird? (small, yellow)
  - What is the bird doing? (landing)
  - How did the bird it? (gently)
  - Where did the bird do it? (on a branch)
  - When did the bird do it? (this morning)

❑ Use the ideas the students come up with to write a sentence with elaboration. For example, "The small, yellow bird landed gently on the branch this morning." Explain that using these question stems helps create a more interesting sentence.

Read Aloud Activity

❑ Tell students you are going to read the book *Little Red Writing* by Joan Holub, which is about a little pencil going through the many perils of writing a story. Tell students to listen for added details and descriptive words in the story.

❑ Distribute the Read Aloud Reflection page (Handout 3.4). Direct students to carefully consider and answer the questions. Introduce the idea of a word splash which is a brainstorm of words that are connected to the idea. When students have finished, discuss responses as a whole group. Allow students time to share what they wrote on their word splash to elaborate the idea of love.

Handout 3.4: Read Aloud Reflection
Little Red Writing by Joan Holub

Name: _____

Summarize the main idea of "Little Red Writing".	How did the character show elaboration?

Adding a little bit of color!
Little Red adds color to her story using elaboration.
Create a word splash to elaborate on the idea of love.

Box 3.2: *Little Red Writing*
Key Understandings

❑ In a classroom of pencils, the teacher assigns each pencil to write a story. Little Red, a red pencil, decides she is going to write a story about bravery, since red is the color of bravery. Little Red is given a basket of nouns and sets out on her journey to write a story. She wanders the story path meeting descriptive adjectives, adverbs, and active verbs. At last, she reaches the school office only to find Principal Granny, who now has a long electric tail and a growly voice. Little Red quickly realizes this is not the principal but Wolf 3000, a pencil sharpener. Little Red defeats the pencil sharpener and all is well.

❑ The author uses elaboration when selecting specific nouns, verbs, adjectives, and adverbs. She adds many details throughout the story to develop a strong descriptive storyline.

Skill Development Activity

Objective: Discover how authors use elaboration when writing.

❑ Hand out a lollipop to each student. Tell students to observe their lollipop and think about ways to describe it. Have students turn to a partner and describe their lollipop. Ask probing questions using their senses: How does it look, feel, smell, taste?

❑ Tell students you will be creating a shared writing piece about lollipops. Display the Elaboration Pre-Writing Chart (Handout 3.5). Explain that the topic sentence provides the structure for the rest of the paragraph. Ask students for suggestions for the topic sentence and then model writing a complete topic sentence. For example, "Lollipops are a type of candy that come in a variety of flavors, shapes, and sizes."

❑ Ask students, "What information or ideas support the topic sentence?" Guide students to the supporting ideas. On this chart, model jotting down bullet points. Tell students they will turn the ideas into full sentences later. Ask students to support the topic sentence with a detail, for example:

Handout 3.5: Elaboration Pre-writing Chart

Name: _____

Topic Sentence: _____

_____

_____

Idea	So What? Why is that important?

Closing Sentence: _____

_____

_____

Handout 3.6: Paragraph Frame

Name: _____

Topic Sentence: _____
_____
_____

Idea 1:

Why is this important? Who cares about this? Why does that matter?

Idea 2:

Why is this important? Who cares about this? Why does that matter?

Idea 3:

Why is this important? Who cares about this? Why does that matter?

Closing Sentence: _____
_____
_____

- ❏ Idea 1: "Lollipops come in many flavors."
- ❏ Tell students that to write a strong paragraph, you need to elaborate on the details. At this point, introduce the elaboration sentence prompts. ("So what?" and "why is this important?") Have students brainstorm and share ideas about why different flavors matter. For example, you could ask:
  - ■ Why is it important that lollipops come in different flavors?
  - ■ So what if there are different flavors?
  - ■ Why does it matter that they come in different flavors?
- ❏ Allow students time to provide ideas. Model writing bullet points which elaborate on the idea that lollipops come in a variety of flavors. For example, "people like options."
- ❏ Continue guiding students through the process of producing supporting ideas and elaborating to defend their ideas. Let the students guide the writing but make sure they stay on the topic provided by the topic sentence. Here are some examples:
  - ■ Idea 2: Different types of lollipops like Tootsie pops and Blow pops.
    - ○ So what? Two treats for the price of one.
  - ■ Idea 3: Come in many sizes and shapes.
    - ○ So what? Some are tiny and some are giant, or shaped like a ring pop.
    - ○ Why is this important? It increases interest and business.
- ❏ Finally, model how to rewrite the topic sentence as a closing sentence.
- ❏ Next, model taking the bullet points and turning them into complete sentences. Ask students to generate the sentences. If they need more support, you can guide them using the example below or one you create.

TABLE 3.2
Example of the Elaboration Pre-Writing Chart Completed

Topic Sentence: Lollipops are a type of candy that comes in a variety of flavors, shapes, and sizes.	
Idea	**So what? Why is this important?**
❏ Many flavors	❏ People like options
❏ Tootsie pops or Blow pops	❏ Two treats in one
❏ Come in many sizes and shapes	❏ Tiny Dum Dums to giant swirl lollipops
Closing Sentence: The variety in lollipops over the years has kept people interested and coming back for more.	

❏ Remind students that when you write a paragraph you must first indent. On a sheet of chart paper or using a document camera, model indenting and write the topic sentence. Continue turning both the idea bullets and the elaborative details bullets into complete sentences.

Box 3.3: Example of Elaborative Paragraph

Lollipops are a type of candy that come in a variety of flavors, shapes, and sizes. They come in a wide variety of flavors. People like to have choices in their flavors of candy. Having a lot of flavors to choose from appeals to more consumers. Some lollipops have a different candy in the center. A lot of people may like having two treats for the price of one. People want a tootsie roll to eat or gum to chew after the lollipop is gone. Lollipops also come in different shapes and sizes. They can vary from a tiny Dum Dum to a giant swirl lollipop. Some lollipops are in the shapes of rings or baby bottles. Manufacturers probably do this to increase interest in their product. The variety in lollipops over the years has kept people interested and coming back for more.

Elaborating Authentic Application Activity: Using Elaboration in Opinion Writing

Objective: Students add descriptive detail to a piece of writing to bring the story alive.

Materials

❏ Image of horses, link: https://unsplash.com/photos/Vyf873nsaxs
❏ Handout 3.5: Elaboration Pre-Writing Chart (one per student)
❏ Optional Handout 3.6: Elaboration Paragraph Frame (for those who need more structure)

Whole Group Introduction

❏ Ask students to describe what it means to elaborate in writing. Remind them that elaboration requires adding details or expanding on an idea.

It is the ability to build up and embellish ideas to make the idea more interesting.

❑ Students will practice writing a sentence with elaboration using a new picture. Display a picture of a horse or use the link listed in the materials section to access a sample picture with the sentence "These are horses."

- Is this a sentence? Yes, it has a subject and a verb.
- Is it interesting? No.
- Would someone who is not looking at this picture be able to describe the horse? No.

❑ Have students help you write a better, more descriptive sentence. Use the following question stems:

- What adjectives describe the setting? (beach)
- What adjectives describe the horses? (strong and beautiful)
- What are the horses doing? (galloping)
- How are the horses doing it? (vividly)
- Where did the horses do it? (ocean's wake)
- When did the horses do it? (evening dusk)

❑ Use the ideas the students come up with to write a sentence with elaboration. For example, "The strong and beautiful horses gallop vividly across in the ocean's wake in the evening dusk."

Skill Development Activity

❑ Revisit the shared writing piece on lollipops noting the topic sentence, three main ideas, supporting details (the "so what?"), and the closing sentence.

❑ Tell students that they will be writing another piece on the question, "Should there be homework in elementary school?" This topic should raise excitement among the students. Tell them that they will be going through the same process but first you will do some pre-writing together.

❑ Discuss possible topic sentences.

- Yes, there should be homework in elementary school.
- No, students in elementary should not have homework.

❑ Next, discuss reasons for and against homework in schools. You may want to record the ideas/reasons the students generate on a class T-chart noting reasons for or against homework.

❑ As the reasons are being discussed, remind students to use the elaboration question stems: So what? Why is this important? Who cares about this? Why does that matter? After providing time for brainstorming and discussion, students will write an opinion piece on homework.

❏ Hand out the Elaboration Pre-Writing Chart (Handout 3.5). Have the students write their topic sentence and three supporting ideas. Remind students to jot down bullet points to answer the questions: Who cares? So what? Why does it matter?

❏ Students will rewrite their topic sentence as a concluding sentence.

❏ At this time, you can either hand out the Elaboration Paragraph Frame or allow students to write a paragraph on plain paper.

❏ Collect the paragraphs and score them using the opinion writing elaboration rubric (Appendix A).

❏ If possible, display student work to showcase the varying opinions of the group.

Elaborating Concluding Activities

❏ Distribute the Elaborating Exit Ticket (Appendix A). Ask students to reflect on their learning about the skill of elaborating. Allow time for students to complete the exit ticket. Use this as a formative assessment to gain a better understanding of your students' readiness to effectively practice the skill of elaboration.

❏ If desired, complete the Group Observation Rubric (Appendix A) to track students' progress with the skill.

❏ Ask students to retrieve their Divergent Thinking Avatar (Handout I.5). In the Elaboration box, they should either record the main ideas or illustrate their avatar using the skill of elaboration.

Bibliography

Bird photo by https://unsplash.com/photos/RLLR0oRz16Y.

Holub, J. (2003). *Little red writing*. San Francisco, CA: Chronicle Books LLC.

Horses photo by https://unsplash.com/photos/Vyf873nsaxs.

Reynolds, P. (2004). *The dot*. London, UK: Walker.

CHAPTER 4

Sub-Skill 4

Innovating

TABLE 4.1
Innovating Sub-Skill Overview

Thinking Skill Outline	
Focus Questions	❏ How could you make that more unique? ❏ What is new and unique about this idea? ❏ How can you modify an idea to create something new and **original**?
Lesson 1	*Discovering New Uses* ❏ **Trade Book Focus:** *Not a Box* by Antoinette Portis ❏ **Practice Activity:** How might we use SCAMPER to create a page for this book?
Lesson 2	*Innovating with Existing Ideas* ❏ **Trade Book Focus:** *Goldilocks and the Three Bears* ❏ **Practice Activity:** Goldilocks STEM project
Authentic Application Activity	*Creating a Purposeful Innovation* ❏ **Trade Book Focus:** *The Most Magnificent Thing* by Ashley Spires ❏ **Practice Activity:** Students will create their own "Most Magnificent Thing."

DOI: 10.4324/9781003267959-5

Innovating Lesson 1: Discovering New Uses

Objective: Discover how innovative thinking produces unique ideas.

Materials

- ❑ Handout 4.1: Innovating Anchor Chart (one enlarged copy for the class)
- ❑ Handout 4.2: What is Innovating? (one per student)
- ❑ Handout 4.3: SCAMPER poster (one enlarged for the class)
- ❑ Handout 4.4 SCAMPER a Cell Phone Graphic Organizer (one for teacher to complete as a model)
- ❑ *Not a Box* by Antoinette Portis (teacher's copy)
- ❑ Handout 4.5: *Not a Box* Read Aloud Reflection page (one per student)
- ❑ Handout 4.6: Everyday Objects SCAMPER (one per student)
- ❑ Cell phone

Whole Group Introduction

- ❑ Introduce the thinking skill by playing a word game. Pose the following questions:
  - ■ What does gentle look like?
  - ■ What does green smell like?
  - ■ What does rough taste like?
  - ■ What does black sound like?
- ❑ Show students the Innovate Anchor Chart (Handout 4.1). Tell students they were just using their brains to think of original answers. Innovating is the creative thinking process that produces new and unique responses. Original ideas are often generated as a result of thinking fluently or flexibly about a challenge or problem. Allowing oneself to think in an off-beat manner requires vulnerability. Examples of questions which encourage innovative thinking are the following:
  - ■ What else?
  - ■ How could you make that more unique?
  - ■ How can you (change/combine) _____ and _____ to make something new?
  - ■ What can you think of that no one else will think of?

INNOVATING

ORIGINAL THINKING OF NEW AND UNIQUE IDEAS

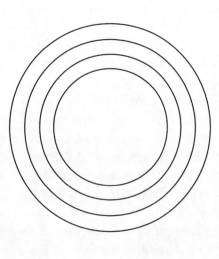

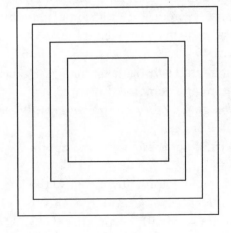

❏ A vocabulary lesson is provided for students to learn the different forms of the word *innovate*. In this unit, the various forms of the word will be used, and this lesson will build schema before students are expected to apply the word.

❏ Distribute What is Innovating? (Handout 4.2) Explain that the word *innovate* has various word forms and, depending on the suffix, it can be a noun, verb, adjective, or adverb. Remind students:

■ A noun is a person, place, thing, or idea.

■ A verb is an action.

■ An adjective describes the noun.

■ An adverb describes how or what the verb is doing.

❏ Read the definitions and sentence with the students. Discuss the sentence and decide which form of the word fits. Discuss how the word becomes a different form depending on how it is used in a sentence.

❏ Tell students to cut out the words at the bottom, determine which form of the word fits each definition and sentence, and then place the word under the sentence. Circulate and check for understanding before allowing students to glue down their answers.

❏ Tell students that today they will be learning a new strategy used to think innovatively, or to help generate new and unique ideas. Display the SCAMPER poster (Handout 4.3). Explain that the SCAMPER tool is useful when you need to change the direction of thinking and move away from familiar ideas. Innovators often take an existing object/idea and change or modify it to become something new and innovative. The question stems will encourage you to consider new and varied perspectives.

■ What might I substitute or change? Other material? Parts?

■ What might I combine this with?

■ How might I modify/minimize/magnify the item or its parts? What would that change?

■ How can I put these objects to another use? What else could it be used for?

■ What might I eliminate to change this idea/item?

■ How might I reverse or reorder this?

❏ Tell students they will be applying the SCAMPER tool to a familiar object: a cell phone. Model going through the SCAMPER acronym, asking the students to reflect on how cell phones have changed over time. You may want to find pictures of how cell phones have changed over time to help students see how much they have changed. Record the information on Handout 4.4, the SCAMPER Cell Phone Graphic Organizer.

Handout 4.2: What is INNOVATING?

Name: _____

To make something new, make changes to something existing

If they keep _____ video games, kids will continue buying them.

verb

Tending to innovate, or introduce something new

Tesla makes _____ cars.

Adj.

Something new or different introduced

The _____ of the computer changed the world forever.

noun

The act of being innovative

Amazon's ability to think _____ put them at the top of the market.

adverb

innovating   innovative   innovation   innovatively

Handout 4.3: SCAMPER Anchor Chart

SCAMPER

Substitute	What can I parts/ideas can I substitute? What can I replace?
Combine	Are there parts I can combine? What could I integrate with this idea?
Adapt	How can I alter this idea/item? What can I change?
Modify	What can I make bigger? What can I elaborate?
Put to Other Uses	How else can this be used? How could I use this in a different way?
Eliminate	What can I get rid of? What if I made this smaller? How can this be split?
Rearrange	What if I changed the order of events? What if this went in reverse?

Handout 4.4: SCAMPER A Smart Phone

S What has been substituted?	
C What things have been combined in smart phones?	
A How have smart phones adapted?	
M What parts have been made bigger?	
P What other uses does a smart phone have?	
E What has been eliminated in smart phones?	
R Have the parts of smart phones been rearranged?	

- What has been substituted on smart phones? (screen and separate keyboard now is just a touchscreen)
- What have been combined with smart phones? (computer, email, camera, music)
- How have smart phones adapted? (flip phone to screen)
- How have smart phones been modified? (various sizes and types of buttons)
- How have smart phones been put to other uses? (Beyond just talking now you can text, voice memo, etc.)
- What has been eliminated? (The keyboards, the antennas)
- What has been rearranged? (The apps on the phones can be rearranged)

Read Aloud and SCAMPER Activity

- ❏ Read aloud the book *Not a Box* by Antoinette Portis. Discuss with the students the ways the character showed innovation. Ask students: Did you notice a time he used an idea from the SCAMPER acronym?
- ❏ Complete a picture walk using the book and having students answer the question: How did the bunny use the SCAMPER acronym to create his (car, mountain, building on fire, robot costume, boat, etc.)? Try to find a use of each of the SCAMPER verbs. For example:
  - **Substitute:** The bunny substituted the box for the base of the car frame.
  - **Combine:** The bunny combined a fire and a house by turning the box into a burning building.
  - **Adapt:** The bunny adapted the box by changing the box into a rocket ship.
  - **Modify:** The bunny modified the box by making it larger and standing on it as a mountain.
  - **Put to other uses:** The bunny used the box as a robot costume.
  - **Eliminate:** The bunny eliminated the top of the box to use it as the basket to the hot air balloon.
  - **Rearrange:** The bunny sat on top of the box to create a thinking chair.
- ❏ Ask the students: How might we use SCAMPER to create a page for this book?
- ❏ Distribute the *Not a Box* SCAMPER Read Aloud Reflection page (Handout 4.5). Tell students they will be designing a new idea using the Not a Box. Remind students to use the SCAMPER verbs to help them create a new and unique idea.

Handout 4.5: Read Aloud Reflection

Not a Box by Antoinette Portis

Name: _____

S
Substitute something

C
Combine things

A
Add something

M
Make parts bigger or smaller

P
Put to another use

E
Eliminate something

R
Rearrange parts

Draw your not-a-box.

Describe your not-a-box and how it is different from a typical box.

_____

_____

_____

_____

❏ If desired, students may circle which parts of SCAMPER they chose to use for modifications.

■ Ask students to write a few sentences about their box and what makes it innovative.

■ If you have time, invite a few students to share.

Skill Development Activity

Objective: Apply the SCAMPER acronym to everyday items.

❏ Tell students they will now be applying the SCAMPER tool to everyday items. Distribute the Everyday Objects SCAMPER (Handout 4.6). Tell students they will be cutting the bottom items out. Next, students will place one item next to each letter on the SCAMPER chart. Students will then explain how they changed the item using that innovative verb.

❏ Allow students time to share their new objects either with a partner or in a small group.

Innovate Lesson 2: Innovating with Existing Ideas

Materials

❏ Handout 4.7: *Goldilocks and the Three Bears* (one per student)
❏ Handout 4.8: SCAMPER Goldilocks (one per student)
❏ Handout 4.9: Goldilocks STEM project
❏ STEM materials: printer paper, clear tape, pennies
❏ STEM Rubric: Appendix A

Whole Group Introduction

❏ Using a household object (such as a whisk, shoehorn, or another common but interesting object), walk through a SCAMPER with the students as a whole group. Allow students to help generate ideas for each step. Do not spend too much time here; this is simply a model to help get the creative juices flowing.

Handout 4.6: SCAMPER an Object

Substitute		What did you substitute?
Combine		What things have been combined?
Adapt		What was adapted?
Modify		How/What did you modify? Make it bigger?
Put to other uses		What other uses does this item have?
Eliminate		What can be eliminated? What can be smaller?
Rearrange		Have the parts been rearranged?

Cut out and glue the items next to the verb you will be using.

Read Aloud Activity

❏ Distribute the story *Goldilocks and the Three Bears* (Handout 4.7). Have students read the story and underline the problems Goldilocks faces.

❏ Distribute SCAMPER Goldilocks (Handout 4.8) Model answering the questions for the Substitute letter of the acronym. Record your answer in the box. What other settings could be used? What else could Goldilocks break? Remind students they should try to answer at least one question for each letter in the acronym.

Teacher's note: Depending upon your students' readiness, you may wish to continue answering all questions using think-aloud modeling, or your students may be ready to work in pairs or independently to complete the SCAMPER sheet.

❏ Allow students an opportunity to share ideas from their SCAMPER paper. Encourage students to piggyback off one another's ideas.

❏ Extension Option: Have students choose at least three changes from their SCAMPER graphic organizer and rewrite the Goldilocks story.

Box 4.1: SCAMPER Examples

❏ **Substitute:** What other settings could be used?
  - ■ The story could take place in a city in an apartment building.
❏ **Combine:** What other fairytale could we combine with *Goldilocks*?
  - ■ Combine *Goldilocks* and *The Three Little Pigs*. Goldilocks becomes the "wolf" and visits each pig's house, eating their porridge, breaking a chair, and sleeping in their bed.
❏ **Adapt:** What if Goldilocks was a good little girl?
  - ■ Perhaps Goldilocks waited politely outside of the house until the bears returned and they became great friends.
❏ **Magnify:** What could you exaggerate?
  - ■ Goldilocks could break everything in the house.
❏ **Put to Other Uses:** How could the story be told from a different perspective?
  - ■ The story could begin with explaining why Goldilocks is in the woods by herself. Perhaps she has had a rough life and needs help.

Name: _____

Once upon a time, there were Three Bears, who lived together in a house of their own, in a wood. One of them was a Little, Small Wee Bear; and one was a Middle-sized Bear, and the other was a Great, Huge Bear. They had each a pot for their porridge, a little pot for the Little, Small, Wee Bear; and a middle-sized pot for the Middle Bear, and a great pot for the Great, Huge Bear. And they had each a chair to sit in; a little chair for the Little, Small, Wee Bear; and a middle-sized chair for the Middle Bear; and a great chair for the Great, Huge Bear. And they had each a bed to sleep in; a little bed for the Little, Small, Wee Bear; and a middle-sized bed for the Middle Bear; and a great bed for the Great, Huge Bear.

One day, after they had made the porridge for their breakfast, and poured it into their porridge-pots, they walked out into the wood while the porridge was cooling, that they might not burn their mouths, by beginning too soon to eat it. And while they were walking, a little girl named Goldilocks came to the house. She could not have been a good, honest girl; for first, she looked in at the window, and then she peeped in at the keyhole; and seeing nobody in the house, she lifted the latch. The door was not fastened, because the Bears were good Bears, who did nobody any harm, and never suspected that anybody would harm them.

So, Goldilocks opened the door and went in; and well pleased she was when she saw the porridge on the table. If she had been a good little girl, she would have waited till the Bears came home, and then, perhaps, they would have asked her to breakfast; for they were good Bears—a little rough or so, as the manner of Bears is, but for all that very good-natured and hospitable. But she was an impudent, bad little girl, and set about helping herself.

So first, she tasted the porridge of the Great, Huge Bear, and that was too hot for her; and she said a bad word about that. Then she tasted the porridge of the Middle Bear, and that was too cold for her; and she said a bad word about that too. Then she went to the porridge of the Little, Small, Wee Bear, and tasted that; and that was neither too hot, nor too cold, but just right. She liked it so well, that she ate it all up.

Then Goldilocks sat down in the chair of the Great, Huge Bear, and that was too hard for her. Then she sat down in the chair of the Middle Bear, and that was too soft for her. Then she sat down in the chair of the Little, Small, Wee Bear, and that was neither too hard, nor too soft, but just right. So, she seated herself in it, and there she sat until the bottom of the chair came out, and down she came, plump upon the ground.

Then Goldilocks went upstairs into the bedchamber in which the three Bears slept. First, she lay down upon the bed of the Great, Huge Bear; but that was too high at the head for her. Next, she lay down upon the bed of the Middle Bear; and that was too high at the foot for her. Then she lay down upon the bed of the Little, Small, Wee Bear;

and that was neither too high at the head, nor at the foot, but just right. So, she covered herself up comfortably and lay there until she fell fast asleep.

By this time, the Three Bears thought their porridge would be cool enough; so, they came home to breakfast. Now Goldilocks had left the spoon of the Great, Huge Bear, standing in his porridge. "Somebody has been at my porridge!" said the Great, Huge Bear, in his great, rough, gruff voice.

And when the Middle Bear looked at his, he saw that the spoon was standing in it too. "Somebody has been at my porridge!" said the Middle Bear in his middle voice.

Then the Little, Small, Wee Bear looked at his, and there was the spoon in the porridge-pot, but the porridge was all gone. "Somebody has been at my porridge and has eaten it all up!" said the Little, Small, Wee Bear, in his little, small, wee voice.

Upon this the Three Bears, seeing that someone had entered their house, and eaten up the Little, Small, Wee Bear's breakfast, began to look about them. Now Goldilocks had not put the hard cushion straight when she rose from the chair of the Great, Huge Bear.

"Somebody has been sitting in my chair!" said the Great, Huge Bear, in his great, rough, gruff voice.

And little Goldilocks had squatted down the soft cushion of the Middle Bear.

"Somebody has been sitting in my chair!" said the Middle Bear, in his middle voice.

And you know what Goldilocks had done to the third chair. "Somebody has been sitting in my chair and has sat the bottom out of it!" said the Little, Small, Wee Bear, in his little, small, wee voice.

Then the Three Bears thought it necessary that they should make farther search, so they went upstairs into their bedchamber. Now Goldilocks had pulled the pillow of the Great, Huge Bear, out of its place. "Somebody has been lying in my bed!" said the Great, Huge Bear, in his great, rough, gruff voice.

And Goldilocks had pulled the bolster of the Middle Bear out of its place. "Somebody has been lying in my bed!" said the Middle Bear, in his middle voice.

And when the Little, Small, Wee Bear came to look at his bed, there was the bolster in its place; and the pillow in its place upon the bolster; and upon the pillow was Goldilocks' little head,–which was not in its place, for she had no business there. "Somebody has been lying in my bed,–and here she is!" said the Little, Small, Wee Bear, in his little, small, wee voice.

Handout 4.7, continued: *Goldilocks & the Three Bears*

Little Goldilocks had heard in her sleep the great, rough, gruff voice of the Great, Huge Bear; but she was so fast asleep that it was no more to her than the roaring of wind, or the rumbling of thunder. And she had heard the middle voice, of the Middle Bear, but it was only as if she had heard someone speaking in a dream. But when she heard the little, small, wee voice of the Little, Small, Wee Bear, it was so sharp, and so shrill, that it awakened her at once.

Up she started; and when she saw the Three Bears on one side of the bed, she tumbled herself out at the other, and ran to the window. Now the window was open, because the Bears, like good, tidy Bears, as they were, always opened their bedchamber window when they got up in the morning. Out little Goldilocks jumped; and whether she broke her neck in the fall; or ran into the wood and was lost there; or found her way out of the wood, I cannot tell, but the Three Bears never saw anything more of her.

Handout 4.8: SCAMPER a Story

Name: _____

Use the SCAMPER acronym to generate new and unique ideas. Use the following questions to help generate ideas for a new Goldilocks and the Three Bears story.

Substitute What other settings could be used? Can you replace the Goldilocks with another character? Can you replace something with something else?	
Combine Can you combine another fairytale with this story? How can you combine this idea with other ideas?	
Adapt How can you change some of the characters to develop a new story? What ideas can you borrow from other fairytales? What if Goldilocks was good?	
Modify, Magnify, or Minify What could you exaggerate? What could you make smaller to change the story? How can you elaborate on this idea?	
Put to Other Uses How can you put these objects or ideas to another use? Besides writing, how else could you present a new fairytale? How would the story be told from a different perspective?	
Eliminate How might I eliminate a portion of the story? What changes would then occur?	
Reverse or Rearrange What would happen if the problem or situation was reversed or rearranged? What would happen if the Bears were home when Goldilocks showed up?	

Handout 4.9: *Goldilocks Creates a Chair STEM*

Name: _____

THE CHALLENGE

Help Goldilocks create a chair to replace the one she broke. You have 10 sheets of paper and tape to design this chair. The chair that withstands the most weight wins.

Step 1: Ask
What problem are you trying to solve?

Step 2: Imagine/Plan
Brainstorm ways to solve this problem.

Step 3: Create
Sketch your design here.

Step 4: Test
Test your design, explain what happens. Record results.

Step 5: Review/Revise
What modifications can you make to your design? What did you learn from this design challenge?

❏ **Eliminate:** How might I eliminate a portion of the story? What changes would then occur?
  - Instead of going on a long walk, the three bears could just be in the backyard. Then they would hear Goldilocks and stop her before she breaks their things.

❏ **Rearrange:** What would happen if the bears were home when Goldilocks showed up?
  - Perhaps the bears are mean in the story, and when Goldilocks comes to visit, they eat her.

Skill Development Activity

Objective: Use innovative skills to solve a problem for Goldilocks.

❏ This STEM activity invites students to use their creative minds to think like an engineer and problem-solver to solve a "real life" fairytale problem.

❏ This challenge follows the STEM format of Ask, Imagine/Plan, Create, Test, and Improve.
  - **Ask:** Students ask questions to define the problem in need of a solution.
  - **Imagine/Plan:** Students generate many ideas using the SCAMPER strategy. Try to get past the obvious solutions.
  - **Create:** Students choose their solution and begin designing/constructing it.
  - **Test:** Students test their product to see if it works. Record results.
  - **Review/Revise:** Students evaluate their design, begin to modify the products, and possibly retest their design.

❏ Tell students their challenge: Goldilocks breaks a lot of the Bears' items. In this challenge you will create a chair to replace the one she broke. You have 10 sheets of paper and 2 feet of tape to design this chair. The chair that withstands the most weight wins.
  - **Ask:** What problem are you trying to solve?
  - **Imagine/Plan:** Look at the SCAMPER anchor chart. What are ways we can use the SCAMPER tool to help design the new chair?
  - **Create:** Students create their chair.
  - **Test:** Give students pennies to see how many pennies their chair can withhold.
  - **Review/Revise:** Students evaluate their design, analyzing the strengths and areas they would need to revise. If time permits, allow students time to modify their project and retest.

❏ You may choose to have students complete the STEM Rubric as a self-evaluation tool (Appendix A).

Innovating Authentic Application Activity: Creating a Purposeful Innovation

Objective: Apply innovation to create something new and unique.

Materials

- ❏ *The Most Magnificent Thing* by Ashley Spires (teacher's copy)
- ❏ Handout 4.10: Read Aloud Reflection (one per student)
- ❏ Handout 4.11: *The Most Magnificent Thing* Challenge Planning Sheet (one per student or pair)
- ❏ Various arts, crafts, recyclables, and classroom items

Read Aloud Activity

- ❏ Tell students you will be reading a book in which the character also uses innovative thinking. Remind students that innovating is the creative thinking process that produces new and unique responses.
- ❏ Read the book *The Most Magnificent Thing* by Ashley Spires. This book invites the reader to follow a girl who is on a journey to create something new and unique; however, the task is more difficult than it first appears.
- ❏ Distribute the Read Aloud Reflection page (Handout 4.10). Direct students to carefully consider and answer the questions. When students have finished, discuss responses as a whole group. Allow students time to share their ideas for what the machine could be used for. Key understandings for this read aloud are outlined in Box 4.2.

Box 4.2: *The Most Magnificent Thing* Key Understandings

- ❏ A little girl sets out to make the most magnificent thing. She knows exactly what and how she will make it, but after many failed attempts, she realizes this is a challenging task and gets so mad she quits. Her dog encourages her to take a break and then try again. She comes back and tries again and gets it just right.
- ❏ The girl is being an original thinker when she tries to create something new and unique. She uses innovative thinking when she tries and tries again to create the most magnificent thing.

Handout 4.10: Read Aloud Reflection

The Most Magnificent Thing by Ashley Spires

Name: _____

Summarize the main idea of the story.	How did the book show innovation?

Now your turn to be innovative. Look at this machine, what are all the different things it could be used for?

Application Activity

❏ Tell students they are going to make their own Most Magnificent Thing. They are to create a practical invention to solve a problem. They will follow the modified invention process.

❏ Distribute *The Most Magnificent Thing* Challenge Planning Sheet (Handout 4.11) to the students and discuss each section. This planning sheet differs slightly from the STEM challenge because the students are creating their own problem to solve and then are creating a new and unique invention.

1. **Identify a problem:** What problem are you trying to solve? What do you know about this problem?
2. **Imagine:** What magnificent thing will you make to solve your problem? How will it solve the problem?
3. **Think and design:** Try using the SCAMPER tool to help create something new.
4. **Create a prototype:** Build your magnificent thing prototype.
5. **Test your prototype:** Test your magnificent thing prototype. Describe the results.
6. **Review/revise:** How could you improve your magnificent thing?

Teacher's note: This is an open-ended task. If your students require more scaffolding, you may want to generate a list of school problems to solve. You may also want to allow students to collaborate on this invention.

Innovating Concluding Activity

❏ Distribute the Innovate Exit Ticket (Appendix A). Ask students to reflect on their learning about the skill of innovation. Allow time for students to complete the exit ticket. Use this as a formative assessment to gain a better understanding of your students' readiness to effectively practice the skill of innovating.

❏ If desired, complete the Group Observation Rubric (Appendix A) to track students' progress with the skill.

❏ Ask students to retrieve their Divergent Thinking Avatar (Handout I.5). In the Innovate box, they should either record the main ideas about the thinking skill or illustrate their avatar using the skill of innovation.

Handout 4.11: *The Most Magnificient Innovation*

Name: _____

Step 1: Identify the Problem
What problem are you trying to solve?
What do you know about this problem?

Step 2: Imagine
What magnificent thing will you make to solve your problem?
How will it solve the problem?

Step 3: Think and Design
Try using the SCAMPER tool to help create something new.

S
Substitute something

C
Combine things

A
Add something

M
Make parts bigger or smaller

P
Put to another use

E
Eliminate something

R
Rearrange parts

Handout 4.11, continued:

Step 4: Create a prototype
Build your magnificent thing prototype.

Step 5: Test
Test your magnificent thing prototype. Describe the results.

Step 3: Review/Revise
How could you improve your magnificent thing?

Bibliography

Eberle, B. (1996). *SCAMPER.* Waco, TX: Prufrock Press.

Gordon, W.J.J., and Pose, T. (1977). *The metaphorical way of learning and knowing.* Cambridge, MA: Porpoise Books.

Isaksen, S.G., Dorval, K.B., and Treffiner, D.J. (1998). *Toolbox for creative problem solving.* Williamsville, NY: Creative Problem Solving Group.

Osborn, A.F. (1953). *Applied imagination.* New York: Scribner.

Parnes, S.J. (1981). *The magic of your mind.* Buffalo, NY: Bearly Limited.

Portis, A. (2006). *Not a box.* New York: Harper Collins.

Spires, A. (2014). *The most magnificent thing.* Toronto, Canada: Kids Can Press, Limited.

Treffinger, D.J., Isaksen, S.G., and Dorval, K.B. (2006). *Creative problem solving: An introduction* (4th ed.). Waco, TX: Prufrock.

CHAPTER 5

Sub-Skill 5

Giving Ideas Purpose

TABLE 5.1
Giving Ideas Purpose Sub-Skill Overview

Thinking Skill Outline	
Focus Questions	❏ How can we take our ideas and give them a purpose? ❏ How can we take our ideas and turn them into a product?
Lesson 1	*Setting an Intentional Purpose* ❏ **Trade Book Focus:** *What Can I Do With An Idea?* by Kobi Yamada ❏ **Practice Activity:** Creating A New Toy
Lesson 2	*Creating a Plan of Action* ❏ **Trade Book Focus:** *Sofia Valdez, Future Prez* by Andrea Beaty ❏ **Practice Activity:** Creating an Action Plan
Authentic Application Activity	*Creative Problem-Solving* ❏ **Fairytale Focus:** *The Frog Prince*

DOI: 10.4324/9781003267959-6

Giving Ideas Purpose Lesson 1:
Setting an Intentional Purpose

Objective: Consider the purpose and audience when creating a toy.

Materials

- ❏ Handout 5.1: Giving Ideas Purpose Anchor Chart (one enlarged copy for the class)
- ❏ *What Can I Do with an Idea?* By Kobi Yamada (teacher's copy)
- ❏ Handout 5.2: Read Aloud Reflection (one per student)
- ❏ Handout 5.3 Inventive Thinking Question Stems (one enlarged copy for the class)
- ❏ Handout 5.4: Items page (optional, one per student)
- ❏ Optional: Prepared "kits" of assorted loose items (paper clips, yarn, pipe cleaners, cardboard, etc.; the exact objects do not need to be specifically set, but an assortment is helpful)
- ❏ Handout 5.5: My Toy's Purpose (one per student)

Whole Group Introduction

- ❏ Show students the Purpose Anchor Chart (Handout 5.1). Tell students that thinking of new and unique ideas is wonderful, but for the ideas to make an impact on the world, you must give your ideas a purpose.
- ❏ Pose the following scenario: What if screenwriter Andrew Stanton had thought, "Oh I have this funny little story idea—what if a scared and overprotective father fish allowed his only child to go to school, but at the school, his son is captured by some scuba divers," but then Andrew did nothing more with that idea? Allow students time to ponder, and if they don't realize the connection, tell them: if Andrew Stanton hadn't done anything to give his idea purpose, we wouldn't have the movie *Finding Nemo*!
- ❏ To make good ideas *great ideas* you must give them purpose and create a plan of action to get the idea out into the world.
- ❏ Tell students that everything around them was once just an idea. For example, people used to sit on the floor, but someone had the idea to create a chair so that they could sit up. Ask students to look around the room and pick an object. Ask students to think about: Why was this invented? What purpose does it serve? Have students share out their objects and why they think they were invented. What purpose do they serve?

PURPOSE

TAKING AN IDEA AND GIVING IT PURPOSE

Read Aloud Activity

❑ Introduce the story to the students. Tell them this story is about taking an idea and giving it purpose. Read aloud the book *What Can I Do with An Idea?* by Kobi Yamada.

❑ After reading the book, discuss how the idea and boy went through a series of changes.
- How did the boy change throughout the story?
- How did that impact his idea?

❑ Distribute the Read Aloud Reflection page (Handout 5.2). Direct students to carefully consider and answer the questions. When students have finished, discuss responses as a whole group. Key understandings for the read aloud are outlined in Box 5.1.

Box 5.1: *What Can I Do with An Idea?* Key Understandings

❑ A little boy discovers he has an idea. He doesn't know where it came from, but he's embarrassed to tell others about it because they might make fun of him. The boy tries to ignore the idea, but it won't go away. Eventually the boy becomes more comfortable with the idea and begins to share it. Even though some people don't understand it, he keeps loving his idea and it becomes a permanent part of him.

❑ The idea follows the boy as it's always in the forefront of his mind. After ignoring it doesn't make it go away, he decides to feed the idea by thinking more about it, and the idea grows.

❑ After the idea was shared with the others, it became more than just a thought; now it is a part of the world.

Skill Development Activity

❑ Tell students that they will be generating new ideas and giving the ideas purpose. They will each be creating a new and unique toy. Show students the Inventive Thinking Question Stems Anchor Chart (Handout 5.3). Explain that inventors often have an idea and ask themselves questions to come up with a final product that is new and unique.

Handout 5.2: Read Aloud Reflection
What Can I Do with an Idea? by Kobi Yamada

Name: _____

Write a 3-4 sentence summary of the book.

How can an idea follow you?

What does it mean to feed an idea?

Paraphrase what the boy means when he says,
"I don't know how to describe it, but it went from being here to being everywhere. It wasn't just a part of me anymore...it was now a part of everything."

If your idea spreads, is it no longer yours?

? What will it do?
Sound like? Look like?

? Who will use it?
Where will it be used?

? How big will it be?
Does size affect use?

? How can you share
your idea with others?

- ❑ Provide students with either pre-made bags of items to use to create their toy (paper clips, yarn, pipe cleaners, cardboard, etc.) or the Items page (Handout 5.4) which they can cut out to use for their new toy.
- ❑ Allow students time to explore the materials and generate ideas. After 5–10 minutes, instruct students to make a final decision about what new toy they will create. Allow another 10–15 minutes for students to create their toys out of the supplies. If students are struggling to think of a toy idea, you can partner them up or take a small group and guide them by giving parameters, like "Let's make a toy for a baby who is in a car seat." This will help limit the possibilities and provide structure.
- ❑ As students are working, remind them that they should be thinking about various facets of their new toy, which include:
  - What will your toy do? Look like?
  - Who is the target audience? Who will use it? Where will it be used?
  - What size will it be? Does the size affect its use?
  - How can you share your idea with others?
- ❑ Distribute the My Toy's Purpose sheet (Handout 5.5) to each student. Students will complete the tasks on the sheet to record their thinking:
  - Quickly sketch their toy.
  - Write a description of their toy. Prompt students to elaborate further details, including sounds, sights, and other sensory details to describe their toy.
  - Describe the audience and function of their toy.
  - Create an eye-catching advertisement for their new toy to market it to the masses.
- ❑ Allow students an opportunity to share and receive feedback on their toys.

Giving Ideas Purpose Lesson 2: Creating a Plan of Action

Objective: Organize the tasks by putting them in a manageable order in which to complete.

Materials

- ❑ *Sofia Valdez, Future Prez* by Andrea Beaty (teacher's copy)
- ❑ Handout 5.6: Read Aloud Reflection (one per student)
- ❑ Handout 5.7: Plan of Action (one per student)

Handout 5.4: Items Page

Name: _____

Look at the items below. Choose items from this page and/or other objects and use them to create your new toy.

Handout 5.5: My Toy's Purpose

Name: _____

Draw your toy in this box.

Who is your toy for?

Where will they use it?

_____

_____

_____

_____

_____

_____

_____

Describe the toy and how it will be used. Include as much detail as you can!

_____

_____

_____

_____

_____

_____

Create an ad to sell your toy.

Whole Group Introduction

❏ Show students the Giving Ideas Purpose Anchor Chart. Remind students that thinking of new and unique ideas is wonderful, but for the ideas to make an impact on the world, you must give them a purpose.

❏ Ask students: Once you have a great idea with a genuine purpose, how do you get that idea out into the world? Allow students to generate a few ideas.

❏ Tell students that one way to get ideas out into the world is to create a plan of action. A plan of action is the steps it will take to develop the idea into a tangible thing.

Read Aloud Activity

❏ Read aloud the book *Sofia Valdez, Future Prez* by Andrea Beaty.

❏ After reading, ask students: How did Sofia put her plan into action?

❏ Tell students that to accomplish giving an idea purpose, Sofia had to set goals.

❏ Model retelling Sofia's goals and the steps she had to take to reach her goal. "Think back to the story; Sofia's first goal was to keep her grandfather safe, then it became creating a neighborhood park. Next, she had to go to City Hall to gain permission. Then she needed to get a petition, etc."

❏ Explain that Sofia did not complete all those tasks/goals at the same time. She needed to break the goals into tasks that needed to be done immediately, in the next month, and then in the next year. Tell students that they will be analyzing the timing of the tasks on the Read Aloud Reflection page.

❏ Distribute the Read Aloud Reflection page (Handout 5.6). Direct students to carefully consider the tasks and the time frames. When students have finished, discuss responses as a whole group. If students are struggling, you may wish to model this process. Key understandings for the read aloud are outlined in Box 5.2.

Handout 5.6: Read Aloud Reflection

Sofia Valdez: Future Prez by Andrea Beaty

Name: _____

What was Sofia's goal?	What were the main challenges Sofia faced?

To accomplish a goal, it is often wise to breakdown the steps and create a plan of action. Write 1 idea for each section of the goal setting time periods.

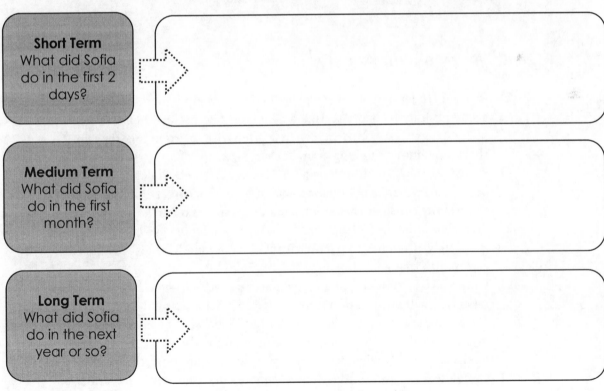

Short Term
What did Sofia do in the first 2 days?

Medium Term
What did Sofia do in the first month?

Long Term
What did Sofia do in the next year or so?

> ## Box 5.2: *Sofia Valdez, Future Prez* Key Understandings
>
> ❑ Sofia and her Abuelo walk to school every morning, until one day Abuelo hurts his foot and can no longer walk with her. Sofia then begins to wonder what she can do about the dangerous Mount Trashmore. She brainstorms a plan to get rid of the trash and build a park, but she must overcome many obstacles to do so.
>
> ❑ Sofia faces many challenges in creating the neighborhood park. First she is told to go to City Hall, where the clerk tells her she can't build a park because she's only a kid. Sofia then speaks to the mayor and government officials, who tell her to build a committee. The committee works together to figure out the laws, surveys, and taxes and then builds Citizen's Park.
>
> ❑ In the first few days, Sofia thought of the idea to build a new park.
>
> ❑ In the next month, she went to City Hall and formed a committee.
>
> ❑ Over the next year, the committee worked together to complete the correct forms and surveys and to build the new park.

Skill Development Activity

❑ Remind students that Sofia Valdez had to develop a plan of action to accomplish her idea of creating a neighborhood park. When there are many steps to complete in a plan, it is often wise to group the steps into short-, medium-, and long-term goals.

❑ Distribute the Plan of Action page (Handout 5.7). Tell students they will be creating a plan of action for a goal of their choosing. Direct students to carefully consider the options: making a sports team, going on your dream vacation, or getting a new pet. Once students have chosen their goal, allow students to partner up with someone who also wants to accomplish that goal.

❑ On a piece of scratch paper, have partners work to generate a list of tasks that will need to be accomplished to meet their goal.

❑ Next, have students decide the order of the tasks. They need to determine what should be completed immediately, then in the next few weeks, and finally what is a long-term task to accomplish this goal.

❑ Circulate and discuss the plans with students, and check for understanding within their plan of action.

Handout 5.7: Plan of Action

Name: _____

Choose one of the following goals and create a plan of action.

Making a sports team.	Going on your dream vacation.	Getting a new pet.

Short Term
What will you do in the next 2 days?

Medium Term
What will you do in the next few weeks or so?

Long Term
What will you do in the next year?

Giving Ideas Purpose Authentic Application Activity: Creative Problem-Solving

Objective: Think creatively and come to a solution.

Materials

- ❑ Handout 5.8: Creative Problem-Solving Anchor Chart (one enlarged for class)
- ❑ Handout 5.9: Mary Had a Little Lamb (one per student)
- ❑ Handouts 5.10: Intro to Creative Problem-Solving (one per student)
- ❑ Handout 5.11: The Frog Prince Booklet (one per student)

Whole Group Introduction

- ❑ Tell students today they will be putting together all the skills they have developed in this unit to solve a creative problem.
- ❑ Show students the Creative Problem-Solving Anchor Chart (Handout 5.8). Explain that creative problem-solving is a process of sorting through a mess, finding the facts, determining a problem, generating solution ideas, judging the ideas based on criteria, and putting the plan into action.
- ❑ Review the Rules for Thinking Creatively from the beginning of the unit (Handout 1.3).

Teacher's note: This activity may be broken down into multiple sessions as you see fit. The Read Aloud Activity should take 45–60 minutes. The Authentic Application should also take 45–60 minutes.

Read Aloud Activity

- ❑ Tell students you will be taking them through the Creative Problem-Solving process and will model the steps using the nursery rhyme "Mary Had a Little Lamb."
- ❑ Distribute the nursery rhyme "Mary Had a Little Lamb" (Handout 5.9). Read aloud the nursery rhyme together.
- ❑ Ask students to *highlight the facts* of the story.
- ❑ Hand out the Introducing Creative Problem-Solving packets (Handout 5.10) copied back-to-back and stapled. Guide students through Finding the Facts and answering the following questions:

- Who has the problem? (Mary)
- What is the problem? (lamb follows her to school)
- Why is this a problem? (teacher is getting mad)
❑ Next, tell students that now is the time to generate problem statements. There are two main ways to frame a problem by rephrasing the problem using the following sentence stems: "In what ways might we help … ?" or "How might we help … ?" For example:
  - How might we help the lamb stay safely at school?
  - How might we help Mary keep her lamb at home?
❑ Tell students that when working to solve a problem, there are often many problem statements. Yet for the sake of modeling the process you've *named the problem*: "How might we help Mary keep her lamb at home?"
❑ Tell students they will be *brainstorming solutions* for the problem. Based on your student population, choose either oral or quiet brainstorming (see Box 5.3 and Box 5.4). Remember to allow for wait time when brainstorming; often the best ideas come later.

Box 5.3: Steps for Oral Brainstorming (Use when you need a lot of ideas quickly.)

❑ Have one person record all student ideas.
❑ Students call out responses to the problem.
❑ Continue to encourage students to further generate ideas by saying things like, "Let's keep thinking of more ideas" or "What else can you think of?" Try to push through the obvious first 15–20 responses. Encourage students to aim for 30+ ideas. Close the activity when all ideas have been generated.

Box 5.4: Steps for Quiet Brainstorming (Use when you have students who benefit from having some quiet thinking time before jumping in to sharing out their ideas.)

❑ Allow students independent, silent time (5–10 minutes) to generate as many ideas as possible and record them on the page.

❏ After the time limit is up, allow students to call out their ideas while a recorder captures all the ideas on a large piece of chart paper.

❏ Next, students will *judge the idea* by measuring one idea against the others using set criteria. Explain that *criteria* means the standard or test by which to judge or decide. For this lesson, the criteria are the following:
   ■ The solution cannot cost any money.
   ■ The solution must be safe.
   ■ The solution must be realistic.

❏ To complete the *evaluation matrix*, students should record their three best solutions under the "Ideas" column. Next, going across the matrix, students will rate how the idea meets each criterion on a scale of 0–5, where 0 = "Doesn't fit" and 5 = "Fits perfectly." Add up scores for each idea and put it in the total column.

❏ Students analyze the results to determine which idea is the best for solving this problem. Tell students that they don't necessarily have to use the idea which scored the highest. If a different idea feels right, they may choose it, but they must be able to support that choice.

❏ Tell students they may each choose their own solution to the problem. This does not need to be a unanimous decision. They will complete the *final idea* page by drawing their solution idea and writing a brief description of the plan.

❏ Finally, conduct a class debrief using the questions on the *plan of action* page. Model considering the following elements:
   ■ Get help or talk to…
   ■ Decide things to do in the short and long term.
   ■ Predict things that might go wrong.
   ■ Determine how you will know if the plan was successful.

Authentic Application Activity

❏ Tell students this time they are going to go through the Creative Problem-Solving process using the fairytale *The Frog Prince.* They will each receive a Frog Prince booklet with guiding questions.

❏ As they read, they will be asked to find the facts, name the problem, brainstorm, judge ideas, and create a plan of action. There are also some critical thinking questions to answer along the way.

Creative Problem-Solving

THE MESS

A broad task, challenge, or opportunity for which new ideas or options are necessary

1. FIND FACTS

Sort out relevant facts and determine what information is missing.

2. NAME THE PROBLEM

Analyze the situation to define the "real problem".

3. BRAINSTORM SOLUTIONS

Think of creative ways to solve the problem.

4. JUDGE IDEAS

Use criteria to pick the best idea.

5. MAKE A PLAN

Plan how to implement the solution.

Handout 5.9: *Mary Had a Little Lamb*

Name: _____

Directions: Read the nursery rhyme below. Highlight the facts in the story.

Find the Facts

Mary had a little lamb,
Little lamb, little lamb,
Mary had a little lamb,
Its fleece was white as snow

And everywhere that Mary went,
Mary went, Mary went,
Everywhere that Mary went
The lamb was sure to go

It followed her to school one day
School one day, school one day
It followed her to school one day
Which was against the rules.

It made the children laugh and play,
Laugh and play, laugh and play,
It made the children laugh and play
To see a lamb at school

And so, the teacher turned it out,
Turned it out, turned it out,
And so, the teacher turned it out,
But still it lingered near

And waited patiently about,
Patiently about, patiently about,
And waited patiently about
Till Mary did appear

"Why does the lamb love Mary so?"
Love Mary so? Love Mary so?
"Why does the lamb love Mary so?"
The eager children cry

"Why, Mary loves the lamb, you know."
Loves the lamb, you know, lamb, you know
"Why, Mary loves the lamb, you know."
The teacher did reply.

Handout 5.10: Introduction to Creative Problem-Solving

Name:_____

| Who has the problem? | What is the problem? | Why is this a problem? |

Name the Problem

Rephrase the problem using the sentence stems:
In what ways might we help… or How might we help…

How might we help Mary keep her lamb at home?

Brainstorm

Generate many possible solutions.

1

Handout 5.10, continued: Intro to Creative Problem-Solving

Judge

Now that you've made a long list of ideas, you'll need to choose your best idea. To do this, measure one idea against the others. Use the following criteria to choose your solution.

1. the solution cannot cost any money.

2. The solution must be safe.

3. The solution must be realistic.

Now list your best ideas and rate how the idea meets each criteria on a scale of 0-5. 0= "Doesn't fit" to 5="Fits perfectly".

CRITERIA ➡

IDEAS ⬇	MONEY	SAFE	REALISTIC	TOTAL

Look at each rating and choose the idea you like best.

The idea I chose is:

because:

Handout 5.10, continued: Intro to Creative Problem-Solving

Draw a picture of the idea you chose. Then write a description below.

Handout 5.10, continued: Intro to Creative Problem-Solving

Consider the following elements.

Plan of Action

Get help from or talk to...

Things to do in the short term:
(NOW)

Things to do in the long term:
(LATER)

Things that might go wrong:

How will we know if the plan was successful?

❏ Encourage students to take their time and really think about all the possibilities. Remind them that often the best and most unique idea won't immediately jump out at them. The goal is to try and be creative.

Teacher's note: You know your students the best. If you think this process is too abstract for your learners, feel free to model it again using the booklet.

❏ Hand out the Frog Prince Creative Problem-Solving packet (Handout 5.11). You may wish to read the story aloud while the students follow along. Pausing along the way to allow students to complete each activity and question set.

❏ Guide students through Finding the Facts and answering the questions:
  ■ Who has the problem? (The princess.)
  ■ What is the problem? (She lost her ball in the well.)
  ■ Why is this a problem? (The ball is her favorite toy.)
  ■ How was it solved? (The frog retrieved her ball.)

❏ Continue reading aloud while students highlight ways the problem changes. Pause at the bottom of page 3 for students to record:
  ■ Who has the problem? (Princess or frog?)
  ■ What is the problem? (The princess doesn't want the frog to live with her; or the poor frog was lied to, and the princess is not following along with their agreement.)

❏ Continue reading aloud page 4, pausing to allow students time to brainstorm ideas for the problem: What other ways might the princess solve her problem? This can be done as a class brainstorm, in a small group, with partners, or independently. A class brainstorming chart may be beneficial for students to see a wide variety of possibilities.

❏ Next, students will *judge the idea* by measuring one idea against the others using set criteria. Explain that *criteria* means the standard or test by which to judge or decide. For this lesson, the criteria are the following:
  ■ The solution must be kind.
  ■ The solution must be helpful.
  ■ The solution must create a win/win situation.

❏ To complete the *evaluation matrix*, students should record their three best solutions under the "Ideas" column. Next going across the matrix students will rate how the idea meets each criterion on a scale of 0–5, where 0 = "Doesn't fit" and 5 = "Fits perfectly." Add up scores for each idea and put it in the total column.

❏ Students analyze the results to determine which idea is the best for solving this problem. Tell students that they don't necessarily have to

Handout 5.11: *The Frog Prince Creative Problem-Solving*

Name: _____

In olden times, when wishing still did some good, there lived a king whose daughters were all beautiful, but the youngest was so beautiful that the sun itself, who, indeed, has seen so much, marveled every time it shone upon her face. In the vicinity of the king's castle there was a large, dark forest, and in this forest, beneath an old linden tree, there was a well. In the heat of the day the princess would go out into the forest and sit on the edge of the cool well. To pass the time she would take a golden ball, throw it into the air, and then catch it. It was her favorite plaything.

Now one day it happened that the princess's golden ball did not fall into her hands, that she held up high, but instead it fell to the ground and rolled right into the water. The princess followed it with her eyes, but the ball disappeared, and the well was so deep that she could not see its bottom. Then she began to cry. She cried louder and louder, and she could not console herself.

> Starting here, highlight the most important facts.

 As she was thus lamenting, someone called out to her, "What is the matter with you, princess? Your crying would turn a stone to pity."

She looked around to see where the voice was coming from and saw a frog, who had stuck his thick, ugly head out of the water. "Oh, it's you, old water-splasher," she said. "I am crying because my golden ball has fallen into the well."

"Be still and stop crying," answered the frog. I can help you, but what will you give me if I bring back your plaything?"

"Whatever you want, dear frog," she said, "my clothes, my pearls and precious stones, and even the golden crown that I am wearing."

The frog answered, "I do not want your clothes, your pearls and precious stones, nor your golden crown, but if you will love me and accept me as a companion and playmate and let me sit next to you at your table and eat from your golden plate and drink from your cup and sleep in your bed, if you will promise this to me, then I'll dive down and bring your golden ball back to you."

"Oh, yes," she said, "I promise all of that to you if you will just bring the ball back to me." But she thought, "What is this stupid frog trying to say? He just sits here in the water with his own kind and croaks. He cannot be a companion to a human."

As soon as the frog heard her say "yes" he stuck his head under and dove to the bottom. He paddled back up a short time later with the golden ball in his mouth and threw it onto the grass. The princess was filled with joy when she saw her beautiful plaything once again, picked it up, and ran off.

1

Handout 5.11 continued:
The Frog Prince Creative Problem-Solving

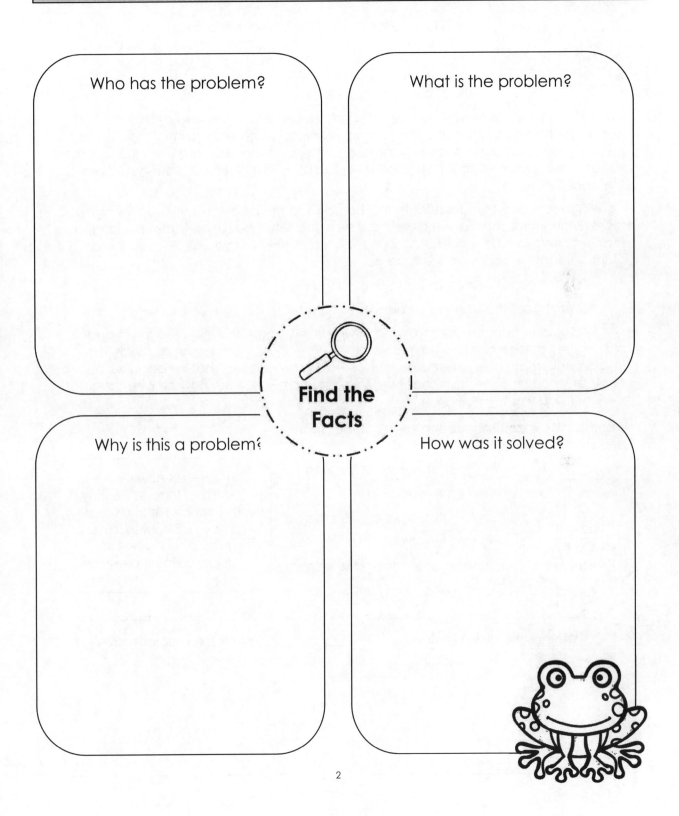

Who has the problem?

What is the problem?

Find the Facts

Why is this a problem?

How was it solved?

2

Handout 5.11 continued:
The Frog Prince Creative Problem-Solving

> Highlight ways the problem changes.

"Wait, wait," called the frog, "take me along. I cannot run as fast as you." But what did it help him, that he croaked out after her as loudly as he could? She paid no attention to him, but instead hurried home and soon forgot the poor frog, who had to return again to his well.

The next day the princess was sitting at the table with the king and all the people of the court and was eating from her golden plate when something came creeping up the marble steps: plip, plop, plip, plop. As soon as it reached the top, there came a knock at the door, and a voice called out, "Princess, youngest, open the door for me!"

She ran to see who was outside. She opened the door, and the frog was sitting there. Frightened, she slammed the door shut and returned to the table. The king saw that her heart was pounding and asked, "My child, why are you afraid? Is there a giant outside the door who wants to get you?"

"Oh, no," she answered. "it is a disgusting frog."

"What does the frog want from you?"

"Oh, father dear, yesterday when I was sitting near the well in the forest and playing, my golden ball fell into the water. And because I was crying so much, the frog brought it back, and because he insisted, I promised him that he could be my companion, but I didn't think that he could leave his water. But now he is just outside the door and wants to come in."

Just then there came a second knock at the door, and a voice called out:

Name the Problem

Youngest daughter of the king,

Open up the door for me,

Don't you know what yesterday,

You said to me down by the well?

Youngest daughter of the king,

Open up the door for me.

> The frog has now come to join the Princess. Review the important facts that you've highlighted. Then, think about what the problem might be now.

Who has the problem now?	What is the problem now?

Handout 5.11 continued:
The Frog Prince Creative Problem-Solving

The king said, "What you have promised, you must keep. Go and let the frog in."

She went and opened the door, and the frog hopped in, then followed her up to her chair. He sat there and called out, "Lift me up next to you."

She hesitated, until finally the king commanded her to do it. When the frog was seated next to her, he said, "Now push your golden plate closer, so we can eat together."

She did it, but one could see that she did not want to. The frog enjoyed his meal, but for her every bite stuck in her throat. Finally, he said, "I have eaten all I want and am tired. Now carry me to your room and make your bed so that we can go to sleep."

The princess began to cry and was afraid of the cold frog and did not dare to even touch him, and yet he was supposed to sleep in her beautiful, clean bed.

The king became angry and said, "You should not despise someone who has helped you in time of need."

The king thinks the princess should...

Choose either the frog or the princess.
In what ways might the _____ solve the problem?

Brainstorm

4

Handout 5.11 continued:
The Frog Prince Creative Problem-Solving

Judge

Now that you've made a long list of ideas, you'll need to choose your best idea. To do this, measure one idea against the others. Use the following criteria to choose your solution.

1. the solution must be kind.

2. The solution must be helpful.

3. The solution must create a win/win situation.

Now list your best ideas and rate how the idea meets each criteria on a scale of 0-5. 0= "Doesn't fit" to 5="Fits perfectly".

CRITERIA ➡

IDEAS ⬇	KIND	HELPFUL	WIN/WIN	TOTAL

Look at each rating and choose the idea you like best.

The idea I chose is:

because:

Handout 5.11 continued:
The Frog Prince Creative Problem-Solving

Plan of Action

Consider the following elements.

> Get help from or talk to...

> Things to do in the short term:
> (NOW)

> Things to do in the long term:
> (LATER)

> Things that might go wrong:

> How will we know if the plan was successful?

Handout 5.11 continued:
The Frog Prince Creative Problem-Solving

> How will the princess react to your plan?

> How will the frog react to your plan?

> Do their expected reactions alter your solution? Why or why not?

She picked him up with two fingers, carried him upstairs, and set him in a corner. As she was lying in the bed, he came creeping up to her and said, "I am tired, and I want to sleep as well as you do. Pick me up or I'll tell your father."

With that she became bitterly angry and threw him against the wall with all her might. "Now you will have your peace you disgusting frog!"

But when he fell down, he was not a frog, but a prince with beautiful friendly eyes. And he was now, according to her father's will, her dear companion and husband. He told her how he had been enchanted by a wicked witch, and that she alone could have rescued him from the well, and that tomorrow they would go together to his kingdom. Then they fell asleep.

> How does this revelation affect your plan of action?

> Does the Princess deserve this ending? Why or why not?

EXTENSION: Rewrite the ending using your solution.

How would your solution affect the princess, frog, and the king?

use the idea which scored the highest. If a different idea feels right, they may choose it, but they must be able to support that choice.

❏ Tell students they may each choose their own solution to the problem. This does not need to be a unanimous decision.

❏ Next, students will create a plan of action by answering the following questions:

- Get help or talk to...
- Decide things to do in the short and long term.
- Predict things that might go wrong.
- Determine how you will know if the plan was successful.

❏ Students should continue reading and answering the remaining questions in the story:

- How will the princess react to your plan?
- How will the king react to your plan?
- Do their expected reactions alter your solution? Why or why not?
- How does the revelation that the frog is really a prince affect your plan of action?
- Does the princess deserve this ending? Why or why not?

❏ There is also an extension activity provided in which the students re-write the ending of the story using their solution.

Giving Ideas Purpose Concluding Activities

❏ Distribute the Giving Ideas Purpose Exit Ticket (Appendix A). Ask students to reflect on their learning about the skill of giving ideas purpose through refining their ideas, considering the purpose, and the audience for which the solution is intended. Allow time for students to complete the exit ticket. Use this as a formative assessment to gain a better understanding of your students' readiness to effectively practice the skill.

❏ If desired, complete the Group Giving Ideas Purpose (Appendix A) to track students' progress with the skill.

❏ If desired, use the Divergent Thinking Skills Student Observation Rubric (Appendix A) to assess and quantify individual students' mastery.

❏ Ask students to retrieve their Divergent Thinking Avatar (Handout I.5). In the Giving Ideas Purpose box, they should either write the main ideas of this section or illustrate their avatar using the skill of giving items purpose.

Bibliography

Beaty, A. (2019). *Sofia Valdez, Future Prez*. New York: Abrams Books.

Eberle, B. (1996). *SCAMPER*. Waco, TX: Prufrock Press.

Gordon, W.J.J., and Pose, T. (1977). *The metaphorical way of learning and knowing*. Cambridge, MA: Porpoise Books.

Isaksen, S.G., Dorval, K.B., and Treffiner, D.J. (1998). *Toolbox for creative problems solving*. Williamsville, NY: Creative Problem Solving Group.

Osborn, A.F. (1953). *Applied imagination*. New York: Scribner.

Parnes, S.J. (1981). *The magic of your mind*. Buffalo, NY: Bearly Limited.

Treffinger, D.J., Isaksen, S.G., and Dorval, K.B. (2006). *Creative problem solving: An introduction* (4th ed.). Waco, TX: Prufrock.

Unkrich, L., and Stanton, A. (2003). *Finding Nemo*. Buena Vista Pictures.

Yamada, K. (2014). *What can I do with an idea?* Seattle, WA: Compendium Inc.

Appendix A
Assessments

Several assessment options are provided in this unit. It is not necessary to use all the options provided, rather, you should choose the options that work best for your own classroom needs.

One aspect to pay close attention to is the indicators associated with each thinking skill. These indicators provide an outline of expected behavioral outcomes for students. As you work through the lessons, keep an eye out for students who are able to achieve the indicators efficiently and effectively, as well as those who may need more support. The intent of this unit is to foster a mastery mindset; make note of student growth and skill development as you progress, rather than focusing on summative outcomes against specific benchmarks.

1. **Exit Tickets:** Exit tickets are provided to correspond with each sub-skill. These are intended to be formative, giving you a sense of students' mastery and self-efficacy with each skill. These tickets will also give you great insight into areas where a re-visit is warranted. If a student would benefit from additional instruction in a sub-skill area, consider using one or more of the extension options listed in Appendix B.
2. **Individual Student Observations:** This form is intended for use for each student individually. All five thinking skills are outlined on the page, and you can track individual student progress toward indicator goals easily. Use this form to gather data, report data to stakeholders, or simply help students see their own progress.
3. **Divergent Thinking Sub-Skill Group Observation Checklists:** This checklist is provided for each thinking skill. This is a great running measure of students' mastery of the indicators associated with each

thinking skill. Each skill has three indicators for mastery, and you can track student progress toward these goals as a group using this form.

4. **Socratic Seminar Assessment:** Provided here is a rubric for assessment after completion of Socratic Seminar. Also included is a form for students to self-evaluate their performance in this unique learning experience.

5. **STEM Rubric:** Provided here is a rubric for assessment after completing the STEM project. The STEM projects are assessed on function of design, creativity, parameters met, and teamwork.

6. **Opinion Writing Rubric:** Provided here is a rubric tailored for opinion or argumentative writing. The areas assessed are opinion focus, organization, development, elaboration, and conventions.

Handout A.1: Generating Ideas Exit Ticket

Name: _____

Date: _____

Generating ideas means...

The easiest part about generating ideas is...

The trickiest part about generating ideas is...

How confident I feel about generating ideas:

Your opinion (feelings, questions, ideas, favorite parts) of this unit:

Handout A.2: Perspectives Exit Ticket

Name: _____

Date: _____

Changing Perspectives means...

The easiest part about changing perspectives is...

The trickiest part about changing perspectives is...

How confident I feel about changing perspectives:

Your opinion (feelings, questions, ideas, favorite parts) of this unit:

Handout A.3: Elaborating Exit Ticket

Name: _____

Date: _____

Elaborating means…

The easiest part about elaborating is…

The trickiest part about elaborating ideas is…

How confident I feel about elaboration:

Your opinion (feelings, questions, ideas, favorite parts) of this unit:

Handout A.4: Innovating Exit Ticket

Name: _____

Date: _____

Innovating means...

The easiest part about innovating is...

The trickiest part about innovating ideas is...

How confident I feel about innovating:

Your opinion (feelings, questions, ideas, favorite parts) of this unit:

Handout A.5: Purpose Exit Ticket

Name: _____

Date: _____

> Giving Ideas purpose means...

> The easiest part about giving ideas purpose is...

> The trickiest part about giving ideas purpose is...

> How confident I feel about giving ideas purpose is:
>
>

> Your opinion (feelings, questions, ideas, favorite parts) of this unit:

Handout A.6: Individual Student Observation Rubric

Student name:

Masterful	Exceeds expectations
Proficient	Independent mastery
Developing	Success with scaffolding
Beginning	Not yet achieved

	MASTERFUL (4)	PROFICIENT (3)	DEVELOPING (2)	BEGINNING (1)
GENERATING IDEAS • Offers many and varied ideas • Piggybacks on existing ideas • Persists in thinking even when ideas come slowly				
	Notes:			
CHANGING PERSPECTIVES • Offers many different types of responses • Changes categories readily • Synthesizes (combines) various perspectives				
	Notes:			
INNOVATING • Offers off-beat and/or unique ideas • Adapts existing ideas to create something new • Uses materials and/or thinking strategies in new ways				
	Notes;			
ELABORATING • Adds many details to both new and existing ideas • Clarifies ideas of self and others to extend thinking • Demonstrates inquiry into unknowns to further develop ideas				
	Notes:			
GIVING IDEAS PURPOSE • Evaluates usefulness of ideas as workable solutions • Puts forth a product or plan to solve a problem • Analyzes implications of various solutions				
	Notes:			

Handout A.7: Generating Ideas Group Checklist

*	Exceeds expectations
+	Independent mastery
✓	Success with scaffolding
o	Not yet achieved

Students	Indicators		
	Offers many and varied ideas	Piggybacks on existing ideas	Persists in thinking, even when ideas come slowly

Handout A.8: Changing Perspectives Group Checklist

*	Exceeds expectations
+	Independent mastery
✓	Success with scaffolding
o	Not yet achieved

Students	Indicators		
	Offers many different types of responses	Changes categories readily	Synthesizes (combines) various perspectives

Handout A.9: Innovating Group Checklist

*	Exceeds expectations
+	Independent mastery
✓	Success with scaffolding
o	Not yet achieved

Students	Indicators		
	Offers off-beat and/or unique ideas	Adapts existing ideas to create something new	Uses materials and/or thinking strategies in new ways

Handout A.10: Elaborating Group Checklist

*	Exceeds expectations
+	Independent mastery
✓	Success with scaffolding
o	Not yet achieved

Students	Indicators		
	Adds many details to both new and existing ideas	Clarifies ideas of self and others to extend thinking	Demonstrates inquiry into unknowns to further develop ideas

Handout A.11: Giving Ideas Purpose Group Checklist

*	Exceeds expectations
+	Independent mastery
✓	Success with scaffolding
o	Not yet achieved

Students	Indicators		
	Evaluates usefulness of ideas as workable solutions	Puts forth a product or plan to solve a problem	Analyzes implications of various solutions

Handout A.12:

Socratic Seminar Self-Reflection

Name: _____

Date: _____

Something I did well is:

Something I wish I had done differently is:

This part of my thinking stayed the same:

This part of my thinking changed:

How I feel Socratic Seminar went for our group today:

Your opinion (feelings, questions, ideas, favorite parts) of this Socratic Seminar:

Handout A.13: Socratic Seminar Rubric

Student name:

	Exemplary	**Proficient**	**Developing**	**Beginning**
Preparation	Student has read the text multiple times, taken notes, highlights key words or phrases.	Student has read the material and has a good understanding.	Student appears to have skimmed the article but shows little reflection prior to the seminar.	Student is unprepared. Has not read the article or taken notes.
Content Knowledge	Student skillfully analyzes and interprets the information. Student provides meaningful references to the text.	Student compiles and interprets the information effectively. Student provides some references to the text.	Student compiles and lists facts from the text.. Student relies heavily on opinions but is unable to support with text.	Student requires teacher guidance to compile ideas. Requires frequent prompting.
Reasoning	Student cites relevant text evidence. Makes connections to other topics. Asks questions to further the dialogue. Willing to hear/take on other viewpoints.	Student cites some text evidence. Makes limited connections to others' ideas. May be able to hear other viewpoints.	Student misses main points of the dialogue. May have some misunderstandings. Limited textual support. Refuses to acknowledge other viewpoints.	Comments do not make sense with the dialogue. Can't stay with the conversation..
Communicates thinking and reasoning effectively	Student is able to discuss thinking clearly, supporting claims with evidence and responding to claims of others. Builds on the ideas of others.	Student can discuss thinking clearly and support their own claims. May build on the ideas of others.	Student can discuss their own thinking clearly. Limited connecting or building upon the ideas of others.	Student participates in discussion and can communicate effectively with teacher guidance.
Listening	Pays attention to details. Listens to others respectfully by making eye contact with the speaker and waiting their turn to speak. Asks for clarification.	Student generally pays attention to others. Listens to others by making some eye contact with the speaker. May be too absorbed in their own ideas to actively engage in the discussion.	Appears to listen on and off throughout the seminar. May find some ideas unimportant and/or may be confused and not ask for clarification.	Student is uninvolved in the Socratic Seminar. Lots of misunderstanding due to inattention.
Conduct	Student demonstrates respect for others and follows the discussion. Participates but does not control the conversation.	Student generally demonstrates respect for others and follows the discussion. May show some impatience with other points of view. Avoids controlling the conversation.	Participates but tends to debate more than offer dialogue or is too timid to add to the conversation. May try to win. May engage in sidebar conversations.	Displays little respect for the learning process and interrupts frequently. Comments are not related or inappropriate.

Handout A.14: STEM Rubric

Student name:

	Function of Design	Creativity	Parameters/ Constraints	Teamwork
STEMtastic Engineer	The product is successfully designed and performed the function of the task.	The design is highly creative and unique.	The design completely followed the parameters and constraints of the task. The materials used for this project were effectively used.	All team members participated and collaborated in all aspects of the design challenge. Team members were well respected for their ideas and contributions.
STEMazing Engineer	The product is designed to perform the challenge task but doesn't actually work.	The design is creative and resembles only a few other designs.	The design followed the parameters and constraints of the task yet did not utilize the materials in an effective way.	Most of the team members participated and collaborated in the design challenge. Team members were encouraged to participate.
STEMprogress Engineer	The product design did not actually attend to the challenge task and did not work.	The design is similar to many other ideas, limited creativity was used in this challenge.	The design did not follow the parameters and constraints of the task. The materials used for this project were not utilized in an effective way.	The team members struggled to collaborate on this design challenge. Team members did not respect one another and work together.

NOTES:

Handout A.15: Opinion Writing Rubric

Score	Opinion Focus	Organization & Development	Elaboration	Conventions
4 **Exemplary**	• Introduces a strong opinion that is clear and concise • Establishes a strong connection between opinion, evidence, and reasons	• Contains an effective introduction & conclusion. • Logically sequences reasons and evidence • Uses sophisticated transitions/transitional phrases	• Frequently uses strong and descriptive sentences to clearly express ideas and support the opinion • Utilizes advanced vocabulary	• Demonstrates command of grade-level conventions; errors are minor and do not interfere with the understanding of the text
3 **Proficient**	• Introduces a clear opinion • Provides adequate connections between opinion, evidence, and reasons	• Contains a relevant introduction & concluding statement • Adequately sequences reasons and evidence • Uses frequent transitions	• Adequately uses descriptive sentences to express ideas and support the opinion • Utilizes strong vocabulary most of the time	• Uses grade-level conventions most of the time; errors are minor and do not interfere with the understanding of the text.
2 **Developing**	• States a weak opinion • Provides limited connections between opinion, evidence, and reasons	• Contains a limited introduction and conclusion • Attempts to group ideas together	• Limited use of descriptive sentences to express ideas and support the opinion • Utilizes strong vocabulary some of the time	• Uses grade-level appropriate conventions some of the time; some errors interfere with the understanding of the text
1 **Beginning**	• States and unclear opinion • Fails to support the opinion with evidence or reasons	• Contains no or irrelevant introduction and conclusion. • Fails to group ideas in a meaningful manner	• Little to no use of descriptive sentences to express ideas and support the opinion • Uses simplistic word choice	• Does not use grade-level appropriate conventions; the errors prohibit understanding of the text.

Appendix B

Extensions

Alternate Trade Books

In some cases, not all the trade books referenced within this unit may be readily available, or they may not be suited for your classroom environment, preferences, or audience. In other cases, you may choose to expand or deepen student understanding through an additional example rooted in rich text. Books listed in Table B.1 are suggestions for further study or to take the place of any of the read-aloud trade books suggested throughout the unit. Also included is a blackline master Read Aloud Reflection (Handout B.1), which can be used with any book of your choice to target the specified thinking skill.

TABLE B.1
Suggested Alternate Trade Books

Divergent Thinking Sub-Skill	Suggested Alternate Trade Books/Guiding Questions
Generating Ideas	❑ *Ish* by Peter Reynolds 　■ The character learns that drawing to perfection isn't as fun as fluently generating pictures that are close enough to look item-ish. ❑ *Lots of Dots* by Craig Frazier 　■ This picture book encourages kids to look for dots and circles in their everyday world. See how many things you can find. ❑ *Arnie the Doughnut* by Laurie Keller 　■ How can Arnie generate ideas to avoid his fate...of being eaten?
Changing Perspectives	❑ *Sky Color* by Peter Reynolds 　■ The character wants to paint the sky but doesn't have any blue paint. She learns that by changing her perspective, the sky can be various colors. ❑ *Beautiful Oops!* by Barnie Saltzberg 　■ Students learn that you can change anything, a spill, a smudge, and tear into art if you simply change your perspective. ❑ *The Squiggle* by Carole Lexa Schaefer 　■ A little girl finds a string on the sidewalk and creatively turns it into many different pictures by looking at the string from various perspectives. ❑ *Duck Rabbit* by Amy Rosenthal and Tom Lichtenheld 　■ This optical illusion book requires students to change their perspective to determine if the image is a duck or a rabbit.
Elaborating	❑ *A Little Bit of Oomph!* by Barnie Saltzberg 　■ Adding a little oomph turns the ordinary, extraordinary. ❑ *Bad Day At Riverbend* by Chris Van Allsburg 　■ This adventure begins as a black-and-white story but then the crayons attack and elaborate the story with color. ❑ *Big Frog Can't Fit In* by Mo Willems 　■ In this "pop-out" book a poor Big Frog just can't fit into the book. ❑ *Sector 7* by David Wiesner 　■ A boy discovers a gateway into the cloud factory in the sky.

(Continued)

TABLE B.1
(Continued)

Divergent Thinking Sub-Skill	Suggested Alternate Trade Books/Guiding Questions

Innovating	❏ *Going Places* by Peter Reynolds
	  ■ A build your own go-cart challenge inspires creative innovation.
	❏ *Meggie Moon* by Elizabeth Baguley
	  ■ Meggie builds some amazing items out of junkyard parts.
	❏ *Not a Stick* by Antoinette Portis
	  ■ What are all the things you can make with a stick?

Giving Ideas Purpose	❏ *Westlandia* by Paul Fleischman
	  ■ A boy gives an idea purpose by creating his own civilization.
	❏ *Iggy Peck, Architect* by Andrea Beaty
	  ■ A young boy brings architecture to life.
	❏ *Apples to Oregon* by Deborah Hopkinson
	  ■ A young girl is resourceful in coming up with creative solutions to help her family.

Novel Study Extensions

Novels are a great way to extend learning about thinking skills, applying divergent thinking in a broader context. The novels listed below support the thinking skills of this unit. The novel study units will allow the students to apply the thinking skills while reading excellent literature.

❏ *The Phantom Tollbooth* by Norman Juster
  ■ *The Phantom Tollbooth* is the fantastical story of Milo, a bored kid who takes an exciting journey through a magical kingdom. During his journey, he discovers that life and learning are not boring after all. He meets a variety of characters who, through their own shortcomings, teach Milo the value of education and to appreciate the everyday things around him.
❏ *A Wrinkle in Time* by Madeleine L'Engle
  ■ *A Wrinkle in Time* is a classic science fiction novel that follows Meg Murry through time and space. She battles a "dark thing" with the help of her brother Charles Wallace and her friend Calvin, learning a lot about herself and about life along the way.

Handout B.1: Universal Read Aloud Reflection

Book Title:

Name: _____

Summarize the main idea of the story.	How did the book connect to the focus skill?

What details from the text showcase the focus skill?

What patterns do you notice in your list from the question above?

What generalization (big idea) can you make about the focus skill based on this book?

❏ *Artemis Fowl* by Eoin Colfer
  ■ Artemis Fowl is a genius and a millionaire. He is also a criminal mastermind with a devious plot involving the underground world of the Fairies and a whole lot of gold. Who will emerge victorious, and what will be sacrificed in the process?
❏ *Rump* by Liesl Shurtliff
  ■ Rump is a fresh riff on the Grimm Brothers' classic fairytale *Rumpelstiltskin* told from the point of view of Rump, the troublemaker himself.

Games to Enhance Divergent Thinking Skills

Many mass-market games can be used to hone divergent thinking skills. Some suggested games which target divergent thinking are listed here.

❏ **Pictionary** is a word-guessing game in which the teams try to identify specific words from their teammate's illustrations. This game supports divergent thinking in that you must try to see ideas from others' perspectives, elaborate on pictures to help provide clues, and generate ideas in order to correctly guess picture clues.

❏ **Taboo** is a word-guessing partner game. The objective is for the player to give their partner clues to guess the word on the card without using the word itself or the five listed words on the card. This game supports divergent thinking in that you must think outside of a set list of constraints in order to connect ideas.

❏ **Apples to Apples** is a group game, the object of the game is to play the "red apple" card from one's hand to best match the round's "green apple" card as chosen by the judging round player. This game supports divergent thinking in that you must make connections, think from the perspectives of others in order to play strategic cards, and give ideas purpose.

❏ **In a Pickle** is a game of creative thinking. The object is to win a set of cards by fitting smaller things into bigger things. For example, a slice of bread fits on a chair which fits in a house, in Paris. The player who plays the fourth card wins the set. The game supports divergent thinking in that you must think both flexibly and fluently in order to make connections.

❏ **Cranium** is a group game for the whole brain. The object of the game is to circle the board through sketching, sculpting, acting, humming, and solving puzzles. This game supports divergent thinking in that players must use their bodies creatively, connecting ideas to try and connect with the ideas of others, and they must do this quickly (fluently).

❑ **Balderdash** is a group game in which the players try to bluff each other by creating pretend definitions for unique, unbelievable words. The game supports divergent thinking in that players will have to elaborate on their thinking in order to create convincing false definitions for the given words.